C000177069

SPECIAL SIGNED EDITION!

BEN PHILLIPS
SCHOOL OF PRANKS

SO RECENTLY MY BRO ELLIOT'S BEEN LEARNING TO READ, AND IT GAVE ME THE IDEA THAT I SHOULD WRITE UP OUR STORY... ALSO, THAT WAY, HE CAN RELIVE EVERYTHING I'VE PUT HIM THROUGH.

THIS IS MY FIRST BOOK!

IT'S A JOURNEY FILLED WITH LAUGHTER (MINE), TEARS (ELLIOT'S) AND EVEN ROMANCE (HELLO, GEORGINA!), AND GOES FROM A CHILDHOOD IN SUNNY BRIDGEND TO TEN MILLION FOLLOWERS ACROSS THE WORLD.

THERE'S ALSO EXCLUSIVE PRANKS, SPITBALL TARGETS (OF ELLIOT'S FACE, OBVIOUSLY), COMIC STRIPS, GUIDES TO CREATING YOUR OWN VIDEOS AND MUCH MORE.

NOW, IF YOU'RE SITTING COMFORTABLY, FOLLOW ME INTO MY WONDERFUL WORLD AND ELLIOT'S 💩 JOURNEY... SORRY BRO!

BEN PHILLIPS

SChOOL OF PranKS

THE ULTIMATE PRANKING EDUCATION

BLINK
bringing you closer

PUBLISHED BY BLINK PUBLISHING
THE PLAZA
535 KINGS ROAD
CHELSEA HARBOUR
LONDON, SW10 0SZ

WWW.BLINKPUBLISHING.CO.UK

FACEBOOK.COM/BLINKPUBLISHING
TWITTER.COM/BLINKPUBLISHING

MAIN EDITION – 978-1-788701-13-6
EBOOK – 978-1-788701-14-3

ALL RIGHTS RESERVED. NO PART OF THE PUBLICATION MAY BE REPRODUCED, STORED IN A RETRIEVAL SYSTEM,
TRANSMITTED OR CIRCULATED IN ANY FORM OR BY ANY MEANS, ELECTRONIC, MECHANICAL, PHOTOCOPYING,
RECORDING OR OTHERWISE, WITHOUT PRIOR PERMISSION IN WRITING OF THE PUBLISHER.

A CIP CATALOGUE OF THIS BOOK IS AVAILABLE FROM THE BRITISH LIBRARY.

DESIGN BY STEVE LEARD
PHOTOGRAPHY BY RICHARD STOW
PRINTED AND BOUND BY STIGE, ITALY

1 3 5 7 9 10 8 6 4 2

COPYRIGHT © 2018, SORRYBRO PRODUCTIONS
EMOJIS © SORRYBRO PRODUCTIONS

BEN PHILLIPS HAS ASSERTED HIS MORAL RIGHT TO BE IDENTIFIED AS THE AUTHOR OF THIS WORK IN ACCORDANCE
WITH THE COPYRIGHT, DESIGNS AND PATENTS ACT 1988.

EVERY REASONABLE EFFORT HAS BEEN MADE TO TRACE COPYRIGHT HOLDERS OF MATERIAL REPRODUCED IN THIS
BOOK, BUT IF ANY HAVE BEEN INADVERTENTLY OVERLOOKED THE PUBLISHERS WOULD BE GLAD TO HEAR FROM THEM.

BLINK PUBLISHING IS AN IMPRINT OF BONNIER BOOKS UK
WWW.BONNIERBOOKS.CO.UK

FOR THE FANS

CONTENTS

DISCLAIMER
A WORD FROM BEN

DON'T TRY THESE

AT HOME

This book is meant to entertain and make you laugh. A lot. The pranks you'll find in these pages are performed by professional pranksters and should NOT be copied under any circumstances. They're childish, often dangerous and not funny (unless inflicted on Elliot). Despite how it looks, every effort has been taken to make sure my bro comes to no harm. His dignity might be beyond saving, but (apart from some close shaves around the nipples) his personal safety is important to me. So, I'm asking you guys right now not to follow in my footsteps and attempt to copy anything you read in this book (unless your victim's name is Elliot Giles).

COLLECT ALL THE SIGNATURES

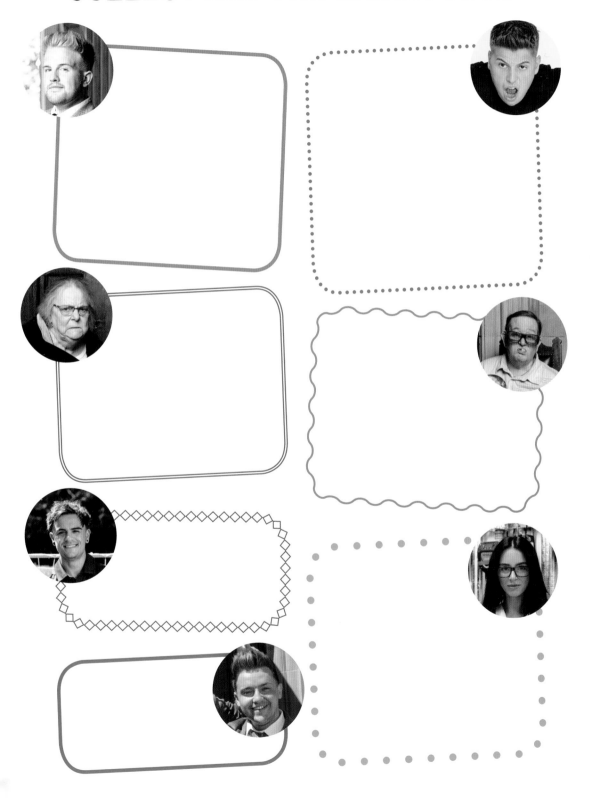

INTRODUCTION

Okay guys, tell me one thing right now: are you serious about pranking?

It takes a lot of work to get to the very top of this game and I'm going to put you through your paces. I'll teach you how to be the 'top dog'.

Let's face it, no one respects a half-hearted slacker, and that's why my School of Pranks will separate the part-time pranksters from the pranking pros. I'm not a teacher to be messed with.

I'll teach you, my students, 40 hilarious tricks: everything from Fart Gas Towel to Superglue Luggage and Magnetic Shoes. Or perhaps the Exploding Candle or Ink Whistle will be more up your street? Maybe you're more of a Wax Pancake kind of person.

The truth is, that if you want to graduate, you're going to have to master all of them. Every. Single. One.

I only want students who are committed to a lifetime of mayhem – if you're a slacker I'll expel you without thinking twice about it. Go hard or go home.

In this book you can also enjoy some awesome comic strips showing you what happened when I performed these tricks in real life. I'll take you behind the scenes at the School, spilling the pranking secrets.

And there's someone else you'll have to put up with... the oddest student we've ever had through the doors of the School of Pranks... yes, that's right – it's Elliot. This is also the story of his attempt to finally achieve something with his useless life and actually graduate.

This book will be your go-to for all things prank... and be your guide to becoming the master of mayhem like me. Now get to class; your first lesson is about to begin.

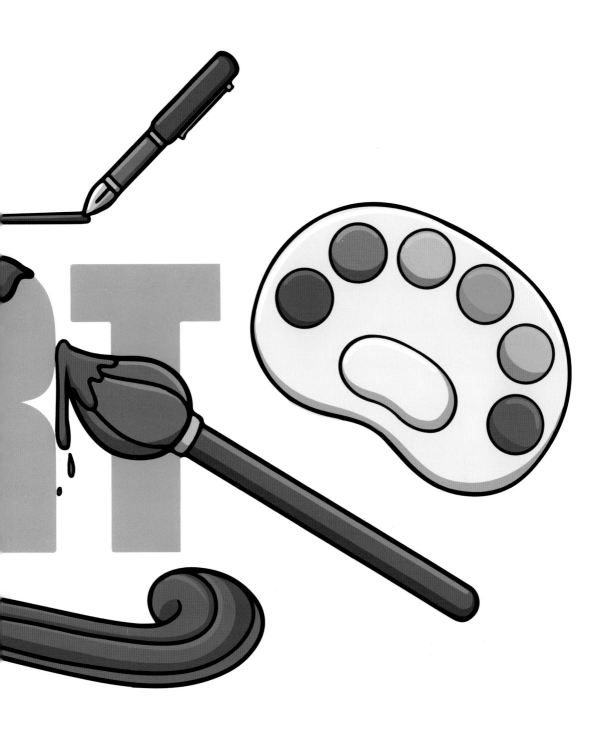

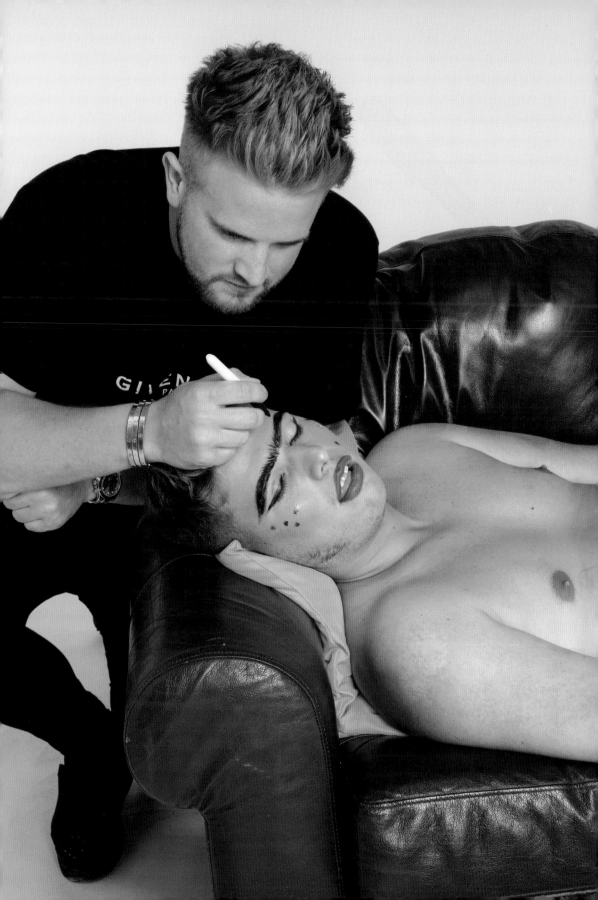

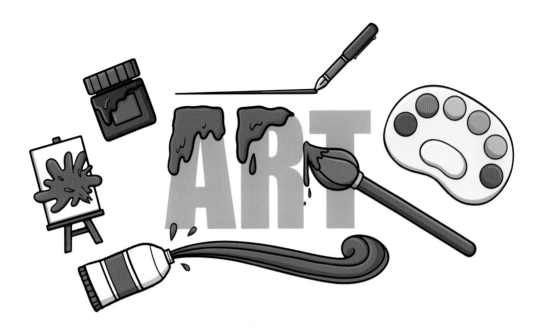

If you're all about the pranks then you're also all about the mess. So welcome to Art – the messiest subject in any school!

The School of Pranks is no different. Take a look through the cupboards in our Art department: you'll find paint, dye, glitter and ink, and tons of other great stuff. If you're even half-serious about pranking, you'll know immediately that these materials were made for chaos. So that's why I wanted to start with Art – because it's a great way to be creative, make a mess and seriously get one over on your mates.

Make no mistake, I'm not aiming to create a new generation of Picassos or Banksys. If you want that sort of stuff, go to an art school and shut the door behind you. I'm looking to unleash an army of proper menaces who are ready to play the best pranks in the world on their victims. Are you up for this? Then read on.

In this chapter, I'll get you started. There's a water bomb that'll cover your target in glitter, a make-up trick to embarrass your drunk mate, and finally, a way to turn your victim so blue they'll look like one of the Smurfs. So, get ready to learn, people – this is Art at its finest!

SMURF BATH BOMB

You can play this prank on anyone you like, but I think that the perfect target for it would be the bathroom hogger. You know the one: the dude who has at least 2,000 baths and showers every day. The nutcase who spends half their life cleaning themselves and the other half hanging around in chemists and beauty shops, buying the latest bath bombs and smelly oils.

In other words ... Elliot. Every time you want to get into the bathroom for a simple two-minute shower, you can't because he's already in there. He's locked the door, slapped on some easy listening music and the scented candles are lit. And you just know he's gonna be in there for hours. Which is ridiculous, because he still smells awful. No amount of oils are gonna cover that reek, Elliot!

If you know someone like Elliot, put them at the top of the list for this prank, and turn them into the creature from The Blue Lagoon.

1 Buy yourself a bottle of blue dye.

2 Add it to your target's shower head or bottle of shampoo.

3 Now you have to wait until they have their next bath or shower. (If you're targeting a bathtub junkie, you won't have to wait long!)

4 Wait for the scream and then laugh your head off as they come running out of the bathroom, covered head-to-toe in blue.

5 For added fun, snap a picture of them, post it on a social network and warn the world that Angry Smurf is on the loose.

PRANK RATING

Difficulty: 2 out of 5
Hilarity: 3 out of 5
Cost: 2 out of 5
Preparation: 2 out of 5
Danger: 3 out of 5
Mess: 5 out of 5

THE GLITTERY WATER BOMB

You know how in the summer some people can't wait to get out in the garden to chill in the sunshine? On a nice warm day, they lie back and read a book, or slip the headphones in and put on their favourite tunes. Bliss! It's like they've died and gone to heaven. Well, those people are about to get a proper wake-up call with this prank. Trust me, it's absolutely sick.

If you follow my guide properly, the moment the water bomb hits your mate it'll explode like an eight-year-old girl's birthday party has just thrown up all over them. It's gonna look amazing: there'll be glitter, water, the works. So, pay attention, class! Here's how to do it...

1. Gather a few water balloons and buy some glitter – the louder the better.

2. Carefully pour glitter into the balloons and then fill them up with water.

3. Wait for your mate to be chilling outside in the garden and then quietly head to a bedroom or a balcony above them. This is your launch pad.

4. Are you ready? Good. Aim and fire! Make sure you throw the bombs quickly and accurately – you don't want to mess up at this late stage.

5. Make sure you compliment them on how much you love their glittery new look. Tell them they've absolutely nailed it, as you snap a photo of them to share on social media.

PRANK RATING

Difficulty: 2 out of 5
Hilarity: 4 out of 5
Cost: 1 out of 5
Preparation: 3 out of 5
Danger: 2 out of 5
Mess: 5 out of 5

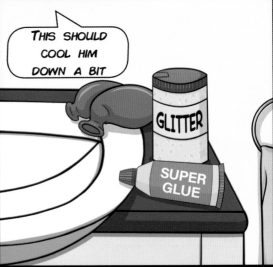

DRUNK MAKE-UP

When you go to the School of Pranks, you need certain things in your bag. One of them is a make-up kit, trust me.

Lipsticks and mascara might have been invented initially for the ladies but they're also brilliant weapons for anyone who likes playing a prank. And, if you want your target to really suffer, grab a sharpie. This is one of my favourites – do it today!

1. Choose your weapon – some mascara, a sharpie or some lipstick will all work fine.

2. Now it's time for a bit of patience: wait for your mate to fall into a deep sleep. This might come at the end of a hard day's work for them, or after they've done a big gym workout, or just when they've necked a few too many drinks. They're flat out, snoring their faces off, and it's your time to have some fun.

3. Sure they've nodded off? Time to move in: apply the mascara and lipstick to their face. Get loads of it on and be as creative as you want. This is Art, after all.

4. Next up, wait for your mate to wake up and discover their dashing new look!

5. Record their shocked made-up face and post on your Instagram for all the world to see. You've gotta share the love, right?

Choose your weapon

NAIL POLISH

24

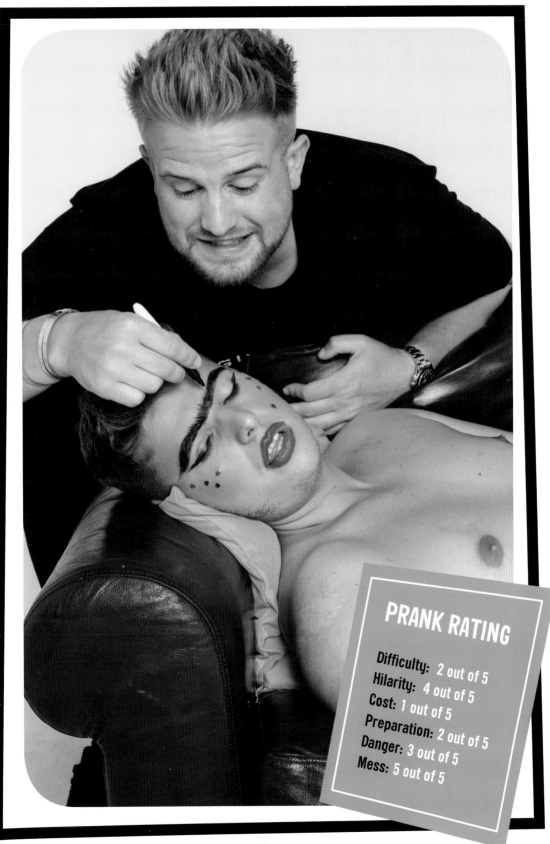

PRANK RATING

Difficulty: 2 out of 5
Hilarity: 4 out of 5
Cost: 1 out of 5
Preparation: 2 out of 5
Danger: 3 out of 5
Mess: 5 out of 5

TEACHER PROFILE:
GRANDAD

'Just step over here by this bucket of paint and shut your eyes for a minute'

Name: Grandad	Special powers: My x-ray glasses
Position: Head of History	Funniest thing that happened in class: Every time Elliot tried to draw anything and we all wet ourselves laughing when he showed the class.
Prank experience: Don't like people to know.	
Teaching style: Old-school – I'm not into your newfangled wotnots like technology, compassion ... or even full sets of teeth.	Top tip: There's no one who doesn't look better covered head-to-toe in paint. Try it!
Number of pranks successfully committed: Wouldn't you like to know?	Inspiration: Justin Bieber, nice set of teeth.
Leading victim: Nana, Elliot, passing cats ... anyone really.	Most likely to say: 'Just step over here by this bucket of paint and shut your eyes for a minute.'
Favourite prank tool: My walking stick.	Least likely to say: Love that dentist.
Strictness rating: Eleven out of ten – I remember when scamps did what they were told and I want to bring those days back. Don't mess!	

HISTORY LESSONS WITH GRANDAD

WALL OF FAME:
BLACK FACE MASK

This is the video that saw Elliot lose his cool even more than usual. Basically, Ben tipped black charcoal powder into Elliot's shower gel and mixed in some superglue and industrial dye.

When Elliot came out of the shower two minutes later (because he's a dirty git and doesn't wash properly!), he had the shock of his life. Then the real fun started as he tried to remove the black coating that covered him. This is a classic prank: daring, colourful and will give you the blues.

In went the black charcoal stuff ...

... and in went the superglue.

When Elliot hopped into the shower, he didn't have a clue what was about to happen.

But he sure did when he got out!

To say he was unhappy would be an understatement.

He was so desperate, he tried to grate it off. How cheesy is that?

The grater didn't work — and neither did the broom!

But the real pain came when we tried to peel it off, bit by bit.

He tried to have his revenge on Ben — but as usual, it was Ben who had the last laugh!

ELLIOT'S DIARY: FIRST DAY AT SCHOOL

I wouldn't say I was bricking it about my first day at the School of Pranks. In fact, once I'd put my PJs and sheets through the wash, you'd never have guessed what had gone down overnight.

These pranks literally had me wetting myself.

I didn't eat much breakfast because Nana said she only had dog biscuits. DOG BISCUITS?! Fine, I wasn't hungry anyway.

The bus took about three years to arrive, but I had no doubt that everyone at school wanted to be my best mate! When I pictured myself in the school corridors, I didn't see myself shivering in the corner behind the lockers, as the rest of the school threw rulers at me. No, everyone was going to proper love me, want to be my friend and definitely not beat the living crap out of me! It's the School of Pranks – what's the worst that could happen?

Weirdly, the moment I walked through the school gates, my knees started to wobble. So, I ran to the toilets for a bit (and because I needed a dump). Once I'd finished wiping my backside and drying my eyes, I knew I was ready to absolutely smash my first day. Then the bell went and suddenly it was time to go to registration. Okay, let's do this!

I tried to move and that's when I realised that I couldn't get off the toilet seat.

When I tried lifting myself off it, I was totally stuck to it.

Man, I was livid. WHO DID THIS?!

Then I tried to pry myself off it but that didn't work either. My head was ready to explode. But I didn't want to be late so I had no choice: I unscrewed the toilet seat and walked to registration with it still stuck to me. I hadn't been able to get my pants or trousers back on, so everyone could see all my bits.

When I arrived at registration, it kicked off big time. All these ugly losers were laughing, pointing and shouting at me. And that's when the penny dropped. Standing at the front of the class, one person was laughing harder than any of them. He looked like he was going to crap himself, he was laughing so hard.

I then realised who had stuck me to the toilet seat: our headmaster.

BEEEEEEENNNNN!!!!!!

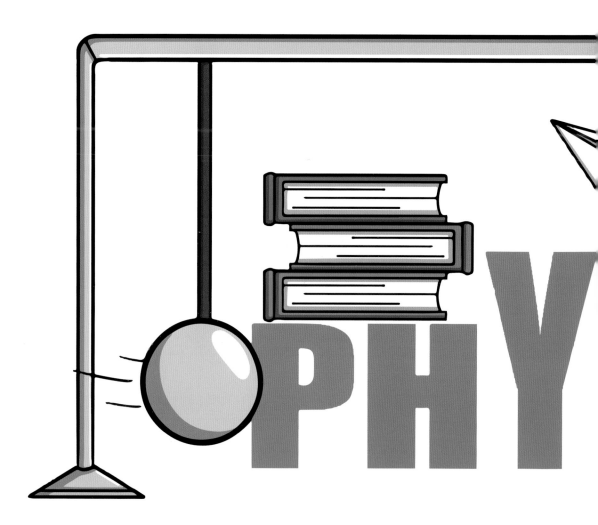

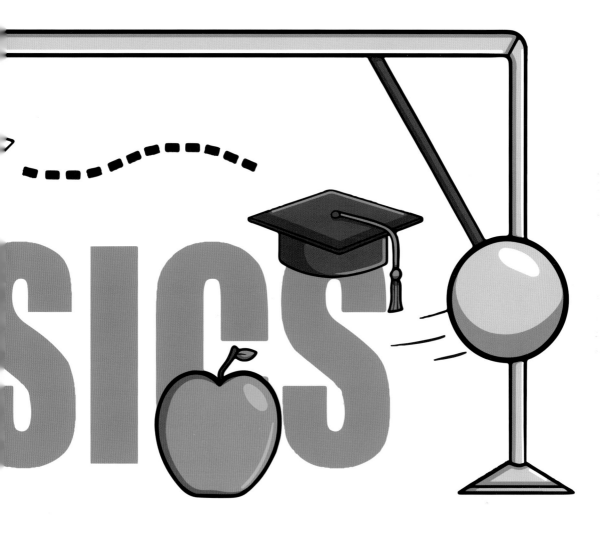

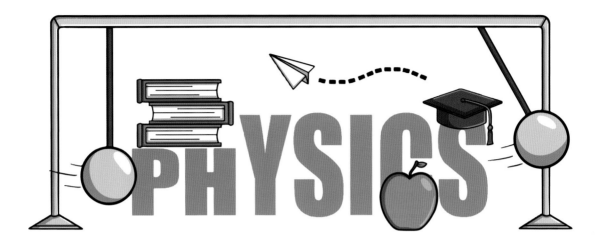

I dunno about you, but when I think of Physics, I think of one thing: wicked experiments. You can have so much fun: you can mess about with magnets, find the most hilarious uses for gravity, even play around with time itself. In short, you can have a proper laugh.

You should have settled into the School of Pranks by now so I don't want any nerves or excuses as we tackle this topic. Got that? Also, we'll be spending a lot of time in the lab, so don't forget your white coats because everything is about to go nuts!

In this chapter, I'll show you how to use Physics to prank your mates. From the Spooky Socks trick to Magnetic Shoes and the awesome Multiple Alarms gag, this is gonna be sick. Trust me, these three are official beauties!

I'll also explain the Ten Commandments of Pranking and reveal the stuff you should be packing in your schoolbag. By the time you're finished with this chapter, you'll be well on the way to becoming a top prankster. So, whether you're a wannabe Albert Einstein or you fancy yourself as the next Stephen Hawking, here's where you can learn to use the basic laws of Physics to play tricks on anyone who annoys you. Let's go, people!

SPOOKY SOCKS

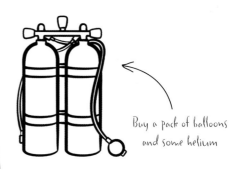

Buy a pack of balloons and some helium

One of the key characteristics about the master prankster is this: we're very hard to trick. You might think you can get one over us on the sly, but you'll have to work very, very hard to nail it. Take Nana, for example. I know that when I'm out, she goes rifling through my drawers, looking for my stash of pranking ideas.

How do I know? You could call it extra-sensory perception, or the prankster's instinct, or even that I keep a hidden camera in my room. The point is, I know she does it and it makes me so mad that I quickly made up a way to get my own back. Readers, I give you the Spooky Socks prank – play it on the snooper in your life!

1 Buy a pack of balloons and some helium.

2 Borrow a few pairs of socks from your friend's smug little drawer.

3 Using the helium, blow up a few balloons about a quarter of the way and stuff each one inside a sock ... be careful not to let them float off!

4 Put the socks back in the drawer and close it quickly.

5 Watch your mate as they go to grab a pair of socks and get the fright of their life!

Borrow a few pairs of socks from your friend's smug little drawer

PRANK RATING

Difficulty: 2 out of 5
Hilarity: 4 out of 5
Cost: 3 out of 5
Preparation: 2 out of 5
Danger: 2 out of 5
Mess: 2 out of 5

MULTIPLE ALARMS

I came up with this one because I was sick of being woken up by Elliot stomping round the gaff when I'm trying to have a lie-in. He needs to get up early doors because he wets the bed every night and he doesn't like lying on wet sheets. So, before the sun even has a chance to rise, he's up, shoving his bedsheets in the machine and making a bloody racket. It's like living with a rooster!

You know what? I've had enough and I'm gonna give him a taste of his own medicine. I've found an awesome way to do it – and you can play this prank too. Just choose someone you think deserves a morning of hell and follow my instructions. You can smash this one, bro!

1. Buy some alarm clocks or borrow some off your mates.

2. Wait for your mate to be out of their bedroom.

3. Set up multiple alarms to go off one minute apart and hide them in clever places, like under their bed, their sock drawer, on top of the wardrobe, etc. Anywhere they'll be hard to find.

4. Wait for your target to go to bed.

5. Listen to the chaos and rage that they have in the morning as they're hunting down each alarm.

Buy some alarm clocks or borrow some off your mates

40

PRANK RATING

Difficulty: 2 out of 5
Hilarity: 4 out of 5
Cost: 4 out of 5
Preparation: 2 out of 5
Danger: 1 out of 5
Mess: 1 out of 5

WHAT'S IN YOUR SCHOOLBAG?

If you're serious about your pranking game then you need to have the right kit. So, let's take a peek together into the schoolbag of the ideal student. Top marks for anyone who slogs around all of this lot!

Superglue	This is such a big part of pranking, you should have it coming out of your ears (not literally, mind!)
Eggs	Ideally past their sell-by date so that when they break, it smells like someone's died
Laxatives	When your bro's gotta go, he's gotta go
A bottle of ink	See the Ink Whistle prank (page 144)
Stink bombs	When a rotten egg just ain't enough
Clothing dye, food colouring	When you want to redesign your mate (see Colouring Comforter, page 190)
A lighter	Another key component
Make-up	If you're a proper prankster, you'll be packing more face paint than Kim Kardashian (see Drunk Make-Up, page 24)
Magnets	(See the Magnetic Shoes prank, page 46)
Talcum powder	You never know when you'll need it!

MAGNETIC SHOES

If there's one thing I really want you to take away from my Physics classes, it's this: the laws of the universe were made so we could play pranks on people.

Magnets were discovered 4,000 years ago when a shepherd called Magnes in Ancient Greece got his foot stuck to a rock containing magnetite because the nails in his shoe were magnetised to it. Or maybe it was because

an old-school prankster used superglue … no one is quite sure. But we can be sure that magnets are awesome and you can use them to wind up your mates.

This prank is the perfect place to start – it's unreal! It takes a bit of preparation and patience, but once your target is staggering around and trying not to fall over, it will all be worth it. I have faith that you can nail this.

1. Steal a pair of your friend's shoes and remove the inner soles. You can choose the pair they wear most often, or the shoes they wear on special occasions.

2. Insert magnets into the sides of the shoes and then replace the inner soles.

3. Wait for your friend to slip their shoes on.

4. Laugh your head off as they get their feet stuck together!

5. Set up a hidden camera and film the whole thing. Then you can post the video on Instagram, warning the world that there's a drunk on the loose.

Insert magnets into the sides of the shoes

PRANK RATING

Difficulty: 5 out of 5
Hilarity: 5 out of 5
Cost: 2 out of 5
Preparation: 5 out of 5
Danger: 3 out of 5
Mess: 2 out of 5

HISTORY LESSONS WITH GRANDAD

WALL OF FAME:
PRANK THE HATERS

Some kids these days think they're so tough online. They send out hate, hide behind their computer and think there are no consequences. Well, after reading one hate tweet, Ben was disgusted that someone would speak so negatively about disability and sexuality. So, to get his own back and to show the hater he was wrong, we arranged one of the biggest pranks of all time: it had zombies, police cars, army trucks, smoke bombs — the lot.

Here's how it played out...

First, we had to convince the hater's girlfriend to join in with the prank. She agreed eventually, and so we hid cameras around their house.

When the hater arrived back from work, he found police and army lined up on his road, shouting at him that a zombie virus was doing the rounds!

After they searched his mouth and terrified him, they let the hater get home, where fake news was playing about a 'zombie apocalypse'!

Then we upped the tension by getting the police round to warn him that there were indeed zombies on the loose.

And that's where Elliot came in. He was all done up like a zombie and running round like a psycho, being chased by police and army!

By now the hater was BRICKING himself ...

... particularly when Elliot started overpowering the police and fighting with the army.

We then sent in a whole army of zombies and also threw some smoke bombs into the mix. Note the detail and effort, students!

After the hater and his girlfriend ran out of the house, we confronted them with a banner of his hate tweet.

He thumped me!

THE TEN COMMANDMENTS OF PRANKING

Here are the basic rules of pranking, the laws you need to live by. You know when God gave Moses the Ten Commandments in the Bible? It's a bit like that, only less beardy...

1. I am the Professor of Pranks.

2. Remember April Fool's Day – keep it holy!

3. Honour thy superglue and thy whoopee cushion.

4. You will never feel sorry for your mate: be honest, if they're anything like Elliot, they deserve it.

5. If you can't decide between two pranks, always choose the messiest one.

6. Never grass up a fellow prankster.

7. Always expect your victim to try and get revenge.

8. Plan your pranks carefully – the more preparation you put in, the more laughs you'll get out.

9. You will not envy your fellow pupil's chilli powder.

10. A prank worth doing is a prank worth filming – and always share the video!

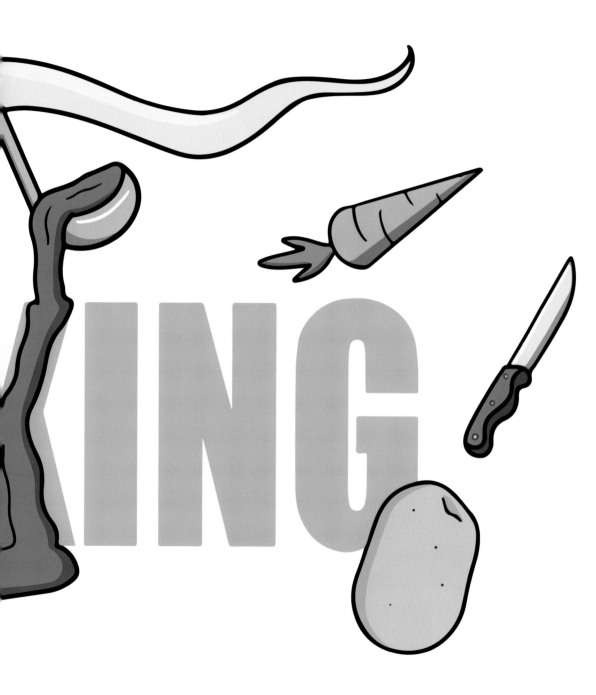

COOKING

Listen up, people! You've done well to get this far, but if you really wanna get top marks, you've gotta run a tight ship at home – and that starts in the kitchen. Food is a top weapon for pranks and this chapter is where you learn how to weaponise it. I'm gonna show you what food you'll need in your larder if you wanna be able to prank day and night. I'm talking eggs, chilli powder, popping candy – the works!

In this chapter I'll also show you how to use wax to stick someone's lips together, how to start your chum's morning with a bang, and I'll even give you a recipe that lets you get your own back on the food thief in your life. It's gonna be like The Great British Prank Off!

You're probably hungry by now so I'll also tell you what's on the menu for school dinners and introduce you to the lady who'll be dishing them up for you: the legendary Marge. It's normally around this point in the school year that we separate the men from the boys. So, get yourself fired up because here is where I teach you how to create chaos with food. Actually, bring your bib, too, because Marge and me have something proper delicious on the stove. We made it especially for you. Go on, try a bit – you've nothing to fear...

CHILLI ICE CREAM

Sometimes you just wanna chill out, but someone won't stop banging on about something. It definitely seems like some people have way too much to say nowadays. People like Elliot, for example.

Every day that guy thinks he has to tell me every last detail of his boring life and then just when I think he's about to shut up, he starts telling me his opinions on everything. There's no point dropping hints by yawning or something, he just won't stop.

What's wrong with him? Why does he think anyone cares?

Well, I'm here to say that you don't need to just sit there and take it. My Wax Pancakes prank is the fast-track to a quieter life. So, if someone won't shut up and you wanna take matters into your own hands, this is an awesome way to do it. Because what better way is there to shut someone up than by sticking their lips together?

1. Buy some ice cream and chilli sauce.

2. Offer to make your chatty friend some dessert.

3. Scoop out the ice cream and put chilli sauce on the top.

4. Serve up. Tell them you put some strawberry sauce on it. Watch as they realise what you've done!

PRANK RATING

Difficulty: 3 out of 5
Hilarity: 4 out of 5
Cost: 2 out of 5
Preparation: 4 out of 5
Danger: 3 out of 5
Mess: 2 out of 5

POPPING CANDY CEREAL

Mornings can properly suck, can't they? You're so bloody knackered, you don't want to get out of bed, but you have to. Someone's hogging the bathroom so you can't get a shower. And when you go to make a coffee, you discover the milk's gone off so badly it smells and looks like something from a cheese factory that time forgot. You've only been awake 20 minutes and already your life sucks!

So, the next thing I want to teach you is how to make your mornings rock. Because trust me, gang, the early hours are a crazy time for pranks. The point is that when people have just got up, their defences are down and it's your duty to take advantage of that and properly stitch them up. This prank is a brilliant example — all you've gotta do is follow my instructions...

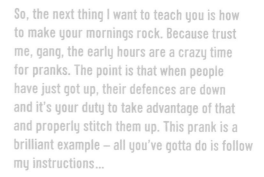

1. Find your mate's (or Grandad's) favourite breakfast cereal and grab the whole box.

2. Get some popping candy and add plenty of it to the cereal.

3. Put the cereal box back in the cupboard and hide!

4. Wait for your mate to make a bowl and watch the surprised look on their face as their morning snack blows up in their face. (They might even spit out their false teeth! Ha-ha!)

5. Congratulations! You've successfully nailed the prank. For extra marks, record their reaction in slo-mo.

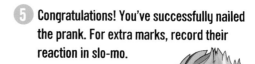

Grandad's teeth

PRANK RATING

Difficulty: 1 out of 5
Hilarity: 4 out of 5
Cost: 1 out of 5
Preparation: 1 out of 5
Danger: 2 out of 5
Mess: 3 out of 5

TEACHER PROFILE:
MARGE

Name: Marge

Position: Dinner Lady

Prank experience: Oh, I've been round the block a few times.

Teaching style: Not being funny, but I leave all the clever stuff to the others – I'm just here to dish out the grub.

Number of pranks successfully committed: I've done more pranks than you've had school dinners.

Leading victim: I know I shouldn't single anyone out, but with Elliot living just next door, it would be rude not to …

Favourite prank tool: I've always believed in the power of a good stew with a few surprise ingredients.

Strictness rating: One out of ten – I'm like everyone's favourite auntie, me.

Special powers: Taking a few leftovers and turning them into a completely inedible meal.

Funniest thing that happened in class: When Ben slipped laxatives into Elliot's soup and he ran to the loo with a brown trail behind him. Took a bit of clearing up, mind!

Top tip: If you wanna prank, you've gotta have chilli powder in your pantry. Go hot or go home!

Inspiration: Probably that Heston Blommin'-Tall fella. Anyone who makes a Knickerbocker Glory out of rejected *Love Island* contestants has my vote!

Most likely to say: 'Norman, get out of my stew!'

Least likely to say: 'Elliot, you're looking slim.'

CHOCO-ONIONS

Is there a greedy pig in your life? Do you know someone who steals all your food the minute your back is turned? You do? Then read on...

You won't get any extra marks for guessing who that person is in my life. Recently, Elliot has been in full-on binge mode. It's like living with a Pac-Man – everything in his path he eats, fat git! That means when I come back from the shops with some grub, the minute I put it down in the kitchen, he picks it up and shoves it in his gob.

It's driving me mad and I'm gonna get my own back on him. Follow my tips and you can play this one on the pig in your life. Teach them a lesson they'll never forget. They're about to get a spicy wake-up call!

1. Buy some onions and a load of chocolate.

2. Hide the chocolate from your mate. Let's face it, they'll only eat it straight away otherwise.

3. Place a small wooden stick in the onion, cover the onion in melted chocolate and leave to set. It should end up looking like a chocolate apple or an ice cream.

4. Once the choco-onion is set, leave it out on the kitchen worktop for your mate to guzzle.

5. Then watch their face and enjoy the tears!

Is he gonna vom?

PRANK RATING

Difficulty: 2 out of 5
Hilarity: 4 out of 5
Cost: 2 out of 5
Preparation: 3 out of 5
Danger: 2 out of 5
Mess: 2 out of 5

#65

HISTORY LESSONS WITH GRANDAD

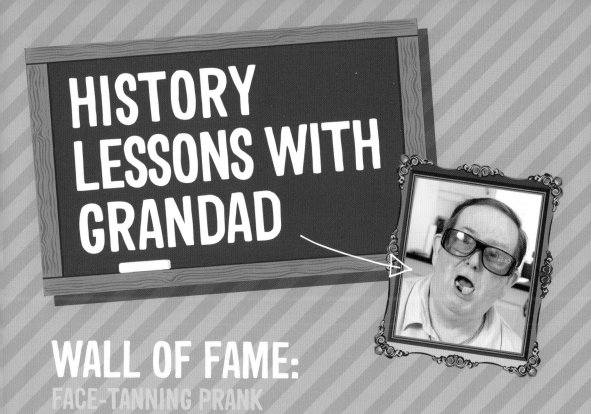

WALL OF FAME:
FACE-TANNING PRANK

This prank showed what a great bro Ben is. Elliot was short of money and kept asking Ben if he could borrow some. So, out of the goodness of his heart, Ben set up a paid photo shoot with a beauty company.

The only trouble was that it was a fake shoot and the tanning mist that Elliot thought he was spraying over himself had actually been replaced by some stronger stuff. This meant that whenever there was a flash, it would suck in all the light and give Elliot a very dark tan! Like that Dickinson fella off the telly.

Talk about a golden oldie!

When Ben picked him up, Elliot had no idea what was in store!

Elliot wanted to keep his T-shirt on for the shoot but we weren't having any of that.

So, topless it was – and Elliot soon got into the mood!

The more times the flash went off, the darker Elliot got.

And because Ben had gone overboard on one side, it all got a bit uneven. But we just kept telling Elliot how good he looked. He didn't have a clue!

Then he noticed how much we were laughing and got suspicious.

As a final twist, we told him he had done so well that the company wanted to make him the face of Garnier. He only fell for it, the daft twit!

But when he saw the mocked-up ad and realised how dark he'd got the game was up!

SCHOOL OF PRANKS PANTRY

Here are the ingredients for the mayhem menu at the School of Pranks...

EGGS

Eggs – they're full of protein, vitamins and minerals. And let's face it, everyone loves a good omelette. Marge says they're great for making cakes. I've also found it's awesome fun to throw them at Elliot. (Other foods are equally good as missiles, including tomatoes.)

PRAWNS

Hide them behind the radiator at your mate's house. The following days and weeks they will slowly decompose and produce the most horrific smell imaginable – and your mate will have no idea where the smell is coming from!

BEANS

The ground zero of every fart attack is a bowl of beans. You get that, right?

SOUP

You can imitate puke with it, or throw it out of the window at your mate. Great laugh! Speaking of which...

CHILLI AND MUSTARD POWDER

Stick it up their nose or just ram loads into something you're cooking for them. These are the key tools for putting one over on your mates.

PRUNES

If you want to give someone the runs (and if you don't, what are you doing at the School of Pranks?), you can't do better than feed them some prunes. Slip some into a smoothie and then watch as they spend the day running back and forth to the bogs.

POPPING CANDY

See Popping Candy Cereal, page 60.

TOOTHPASTE

What? You think toothpaste has no place in the kitchen? You're wrong! You can use it to trick your mates by substituting the cream filling in an Oreo with toothpaste.

MAYONNAISE

Make a birthday cake for your mate but instead of putting cream in it, use mayo. Make sure you're filming as they chomp into it. Ha-ha, happy birthday, bro!

HOMEWORK

Listen up, class. Don't think you can get away with not doing your homework – it's just as important as any other part of your education. It teaches you to work independently and to use your time wisely. Of course, it also shows you how to put one over on those closest to you – and if you don't want to do that, you've come to the wrong school! The thing is, here at the School of Pranks, we're not bothered about pupils who only want to be part-time pranksters. The people we want to send out into the world are the ones who will pull pranks 24/7, even on Christmas Day. So, if you want to graduate with flying colours, you really have to take this chapter seriously.

I'll walk you through three top pranks that you can carry out at home: Ants in Your Pants, Flour Vents and the Cereal Spiller. We'll also take a sneaky peek at Elliot's diary and find out what happened when he went to the school disco. I don't think he'll ever live it down. Grandad goes down memory lane again with another classic prank in the Wall of Fame, and then I'll set you some homework myself, allowing you to devise your own epic prank.

And trust me: when it's time to hand your homework in, don't try telling me you didn't have time, or you were ill, or that the dog ate it. I've heard every excuse under the sun and I won't accept any of them.

This is serious stuff...

ANTS IN YOUR PANTS

There are so many perfect targets for this prank. You might want to get someone back for rifling through your drawers when you weren't looking. Or perhaps you fancy getting even with someone who borrowed your clothes without asking. Or maybe there's someone just so annoying in your life that you're dying to see them squirm in agony. In my life, all of these people are Elliot. Whoever it is in your life, their time has come: they're gonna catch it. Trust me, by the time you've finished with them, they'll be hopping around and scratching themselves in the most embarrassing of places!

1 Buy some itching powder.

2 Find your friend's underwear drawer.

3 Wearing gloves, pour itching powder into the drawer and all over their underwear. (The gloves aren't just to stop you getting itching powder on your hands, they're also because you won't want to actually touch your mate's underwear. No one wants that – yuck!)

4 Hide the evidence.

5 Wait for them to experience the ultimate discomfort – it's gonna be epic!

6 Padlock your own underwear drawer shut!

PRANK RATING

Difficulty: 3 out of 5
Hilarity: 5 out of 5
Cost: 1 out of 5
Preparation: 3 out of 5
Danger: 4 out of 5
Mess: 2 out of 5

FLOUR VENTS

The messiest place on earth is Elliot's car. I've been to rubbish dumps less dirty and less stinking than his banger! I was sick of the sight and the smell of it and I got so tired of asking him to clear it up – he never lifted so much as a crisp packet. So I decided to take matters into my own hands and force him into action with this particular prank.

This is your chance to get your own back on those annoying people in your life, too. Perhaps it's someone you know who has a messy car, or maybe they complained about the state of YOUR car while you were giving them a lift. Whoever it is, it's definitely time for you to show them who's boss. So, do it with this prank: say it with flour.

1. Buy a big bag of flour.

2. Wait for a hot summer's day – the sort of day when you're sweating buckets and it feels like your face is gonna melt away and your bum gets burnt or stuck on the car seat!

3. Gain access to your mate's car.

4. Pour flour into all the air vents. Now turn up the air con to the max!

5. Make sure you didn't leave any telltale evidence behind by vacuuming up any mess and then lock the car.

6. Now hide and wait for your mate to get into their car. They should get a face full of flour when they turn on the engine and the air con kicks in, making them look like they've just had a food fight with Mary Berry!

PRANK RATING

Difficulty: 4 out of 5
Hilarity: 5 out of 5
Cost: 1 out of 5
Preparation: 4 out of 5
Danger: 3 out of 5
Mess: 100 out of 5

HOMEWORK FOR READERS

You can learn a lot from following my prank instructions in this book, but you can learn even more by creating your own pranks. So that's what your homework is, readers: devising your very own wind-up. Fill it in on the opposite page. Screenshot it. Tag me on Instagram @BenPhillipsUK. I'll give top marks and a gold star to the best one.

To get your mind buzzing, here are some golden rules of prank creation...

1. Choose a worthy victim. Someone with a sense of humour who can take a joke. Never be a bully.

2. Brainstorm
Throw ideas around in your head. Scribble thoughts down on paper and sketch drawings alongside them. Don't be afraid to let your imagination run wild, some of my best pranks have been ideas people said wouldn't work.

3. Get inside your mate's head
You have to see what someone's individual quirks are. For example, if you know someone super-vain, that'll be your line of attack. Same goes if they're lazy. Everyone has something you can tap into.

4. Do a dry run
Preparation is key. When you're in the heat of the prank, everything has to go smoothly. So rehearse!

5. Accept revenge
Once you've done the prank, your mate will probably want to get their own back so take it like a man – and then start planning your payback.

Now, over to you...

#SORRY
BRO

REC ●

#SORRY
BRO

CEREAL SPILLER

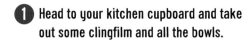

Grandad always taught me that if a prank's worth doing then it's worth doing well. This one really proves his point. Because if you don't set it up properly, it's gonna be an EPIC fail and that means it'll be YOU who's left looking like a donk! So, pay particular attention to step two of this prank or it won't work – and if you mess up, I'll be giving you a big, fat FAIL. In fact, if I'm feeling really annoyed, I might even have to keep you back after school for one of Nana's notorious detentions.

So make this one work, or else. You can play it on any number of targets: people who make a mess, people who complain when you make a mess, or just a mate (you know who I mean!).

This one will give your victim a real wake-up call...

1 Head to your kitchen cupboard and take out some clingfilm and all the bowls.

2 Evenly cut pieces of clingfilm and stretch them over the bowls. This bit is really important: make sure you smooth out any creases, otherwise they'll be able to see the clingfilm.

3 Put the bowls back in the cupboard and wait for your victim to come down and get their breakfast.

4 Watch and laugh. And, just to make them feel
a bit worse, tick them off for making a mess!

PRANK RATING

Difficulty: 3 out of 5
Hilarity: 5 out of 5
Cost: 1 out of 5
Preparation: 4 out of 5
Danger: 1 out of 5
Mess: 4 out of 5

HISTORY LESSONS WITH GRANDAD

WALL OF FAME:
BALD PRANK

Listen up, any prank that ends up with Ben taking a leak over Elliot's face is always well worth remembering – and it's also worth learning. This one will test all sorts of qualities: your ability to prank someone while they're asleep, how you respond on the hop when they discover what's happened, and also whether you're willing to take a leak over your mate's face. So, get the popcorn out and let's all remember what happened when Ben and Tristan convinced Elliot that he'd lost all his hair. Memories!

We waited until Elliot was crashed out cold in the garage. He's a heavy sleeper at the best of times but this particular day he was also sleeping off a boozing session. Perfect!

After Tristan did the 'slap test' to make sure Elliot was fast asleep, he peeled the bald cap over his head.

Even when Elliot woke up, he had no idea what we'd done. Game on!

He even got as far as the shops without realising it looked like he had a condom on his head. How dozy can you get?

He was furious when he noticed, though! 'I look like a half-cut bellend' – well, you said it, bro!

He thought his hair had been shaved off so he tried to buy Miracle-Gro from the hardware shop to grow it back. He started putting it on in the aisle!

It got better and better: because he used the Miracle-Gro before he paid for it, the store called the flippin' police! Ha-ha!

Still missing the point, he bought a wig – a monk's wig, complete with bald patch.

In the end, and this is where it got REALLY weird, Elliot said he'd read on Google that having your head pissed on encouraged it to grow. Well, of course, Ben was more than happy to oblige!

ELLIOT'S DIARY: THE SCHOOL DISCO

As I was sitting on the bus on my way to the school disco, a text came through from Ben. It said:

> 'If you don't get off with a girl tonight I'm gonna make you look like a complete prat. I'M NOT EVEN JOKING.'

Well, thanks a lot, bro. As if I wasn't nervous enough!

The truth is, I'm not very good with girls. When I try and talk to one I like, either she runs away or starts laughing at me. Or she turns out to be a dude. Either way, it's not ideal, is it?

When I got to the disco, it felt like everyone was having a good time apart from me. Everywhere I looked there were people chatting and laughing. Or dancing. Or even snogging in dark corners. The music was loud and the lights were low.

I was dying to prove Ben wrong and that I could find my dream girl at the disco, but every time I approached one, my butt cheeks twitched. Could have been last night's curry, though.

Earlier that day, I'd looked for chat-up lines on Google so I had a real winner ready to try out. 'Do you play football?' I asked her. 'Because you're a keeper!' She just kicked me in the balls. Well, at least it answered my question.

Then I saw another chick, just waiting to be picked up. 'Are you an orphanage?' I began. 'Cos I wanna give you kids!' For that, I got a slap across the face. I was livid.

Third time lucky, maybe? I spotted another chick sitting in a dark corner. To be fair, this girl wasn't what you'd call a cracker. But I was desperate. 'Hey, lady,' I said, 'my love for you is like diarrhoea, I just can't hold it in.'

Desperate for something, I figured it wasn't worth waiting for an answer. I just stuck my tongue down her throat.

Just then the music stopped, the lights came on and a loud voice came over the PA: 'Elliot,' it said, 'why are you getting off with Nana?'

BEEEEENNNNNNNNNNN!!!

DRAMA

In case you didn't know, acting's a big part of pranking. If you wanna trick someone, you've got to be able to convince them to trust you. You have to keep a straight face when inside you're cracking up. In short, you've got to be able to blag it big time – so make sure you show up to the Drama classes. If that's not incentive enough, just look at some of the equipment we'll be using in this chapter – dynamite sticks, talcum powder and lip plump. You know when gear like that's in the mix, great stuff can – and will – go down.

We're also gonna take a look back at one of my all-time favourite pranks: when

we forced Elliot to streak through the streets. It was EPIC! And in this chapter you'll get to know me a bit better as I come under the Teacher Profile spotlight.

So, here's your chance to bring some drama into your life. Whether you wanna be the Pitt of Pranks or the Witherspoon of Wind-ups, here's where you put the hours in to make your dream come true. Okay, guys, you've done well to get this far. Don't let it slip now; the halfway stage is the time to double your efforts. This may be Drama, but it's no place for diva tantrums!

EXPLODING CANDLE*

*DO NOT TRY THIS AT HOME

If your mate's planning a date and they want it to go with a bang, then it's time to pull this prank out of the locker. It's the most explosive wind-up we'll teach you at the School of Pranks, so the pressure's really on – you can't get this one wrong!

I mean, if your prank involves alarm clocks or magnets, what's the worst that can happen? But once you start getting sticks of dynamite involved, the stakes are sky-high – the same place your backside will be if you screw up.

Don't let the danger put you off, though. You've gotta be really brave to graduate from the School of Pranks! Get it wrong and this will blow up in your face, but if you nail it, I'll know you're the bomb...

1. While your mate is busy getting ready for his date, slip out and buy a big red candle, a small dynamite stick and a lighter. The classic Saturday shopping list right there!

2. Cut a hole in the candle where the wick is and slot in the dynamite stick so it's below the level of the wax.

3. Place the candle on the table, lay the table and wait for your friend to come along with his date.

4. Listen out for a loud bang (and cover your ears)!

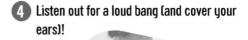

PRANK RATING

Difficulty: 4 out of 5
Hilarity: 4 out of 5
Cost: 3 out of 5
Preparation: 4 out of 5
Danger: 100 out of 5
Mess: 5 out of 5

SMOKING KILLS

Listen up, we're gonna get serious here for a minute...

Smoking really SUCKS. The trouble is, once people start smoking, they get addicted and find it hard to stop. So, I thought I'd create a prank that was funny – and would help people to stop smoking. I came up with this. It's one to play on any mate of yours who is hooked on the fags – they'll never wanna smoke again.

Get this one right and you'll have a great laugh – you'll also help your friend kick a really bad habit.

Everyone's a winner, right?

1 First up, 'borrow' your mate's packet of cigarettes when they're not looking. (If they're a regular smoker, you'll have to complete the following steps really quickly.)

2 Remove the tobacco from the cigarette and replace it with talcum powder.

3 Put a bit of the tobacco back in the top to make it look realistic and then return the cigarette to the packet.

4 Repeat steps two and three for as many of the rest of the packet as you can manage, then put the packet back in its original place.

5 Watch as your mate lights up and gets a shock. They won't be smoking again!

PRANK RATING

Difficulty: 3 out of 5
Hilarity: 2 out of 5
Cost: 1 out of 5
Preparation: 4 out of 5
Danger: 1 out of 5
Mess: 3 out of 5

TEACHER PROFILE:
HEADMASTER BEN

Name: Ben	Special powers: Do you know what? I'd say it's my knack of knowing a million different ways to get Elliot. It's a gift!
Position: Headmaster	
Prank experience: 26 years – I've been at it since I was born.	Funniest thing that happened in class: When I gave Elliot a detention on the final day of the summer term and then locked all the doors and gates to the school, so he was trapped in there for the whole summer holidays.
Teaching style. A combination, really: I lead by example but if in doubt, I just stitch up Elliot!	
Number of pranks successfully committed: 3,982	Top tip: Find the Elliot Giles in your life and concentrate your efforts on them.
Leading victim: Poor Elliot.	Inspiration: Me
Favourite prank tool: It's gotta be superglue.	Most likely to say: 'Sorry, bro!'
Strictness rating: Eleven out of ten – I don't muck about.	Least likely to say: 'Oh dear, I've been pranked.'

THE LIP PLUMP

Next time you're out and about, take a glance around and you'll notice how weird some people look nowadays. You'll see drawn-on eyebrows, fierce orange tan and butt implants. What the hell's going on? People actually spend money to look like that — and one of the funniest features of all is the plumped-up lips.

To be honest, I've never understood why people enjoy making themselves look like a fish. I mean, who wants to kiss a trout?

It's a bloody weird look but it gave me an idea for a brilliant prank.

Play this one on a mate just before they're going somewhere important. Maybe they're going on a date or they're meeting up with some mates. Whenever they're gonna care about their appearance, it's time for you to pounce.

Okay, guys, I hope you're ready? Let's smash this one!

1. Grab your friend's lip balm or tin of Vaseline.

2. Add a generous amount of lip plump to the product (or, as we did here, smear it around the edge of your mate's drink).

3. Place the 'borrowed' item back where you found it and wait for them to hit the bathroom cupboard/fridge.

4. Laugh your head off when they emerge from the bathroom looking like a whale!

PRANK RATING

Difficulty: 3 out of 5
Hilarity: 4 out of 5
Cost: 3 out of 5
Preparation: 2 out of 5
Danger: 1 out of 5
Mess: 2 out of 5

HISTORY LESSONS WITH GRANDAD

WALL OF FAME:
BEN STEALING ELLIOT'S CLOTHES

Elliot running through the streets with just a bin bag wrapped round his waist ... Nana calling him a 'pervert' ... Finally, the police pinning him to the ground. This one was HILARIOUS!

It's a good one to learn because it shows how funny it can be when you really take a prank to its limits. The trick itself isn't that hard – just wait for your mate to be getting changed in a clothes shop, then swipe all their clothes.

It's what happens next that makes the prank funny. So, how does your victim respond? Prepare for some belly laughs...

Ben drove Elliot to the local party store and helped him choose a fancy-dress outfit for a party he'd been invited to.

While he was trying it on, Ben swiped his clothes and ran off.

Soon, Elliot was on the run. He'd wrapped a bin bag round his privates but he still looked a lemon!

He couldn't get into his house because he'd lost his key.

He kept trying to catch up with Ben but he couldn't!

Then he snuck into Nana's garden but we locked him out so his humiliation could continue. She made it even worse for him by calling him a 'pervert'. Ha-ha!

Elliot managed to sneak past the police ...

... but that just set up a new chase ...

... one that he lost.

The police asked if Ben knew him but he said he'd never seen him in his life, thus sealing Elliot's fate. What a donk!

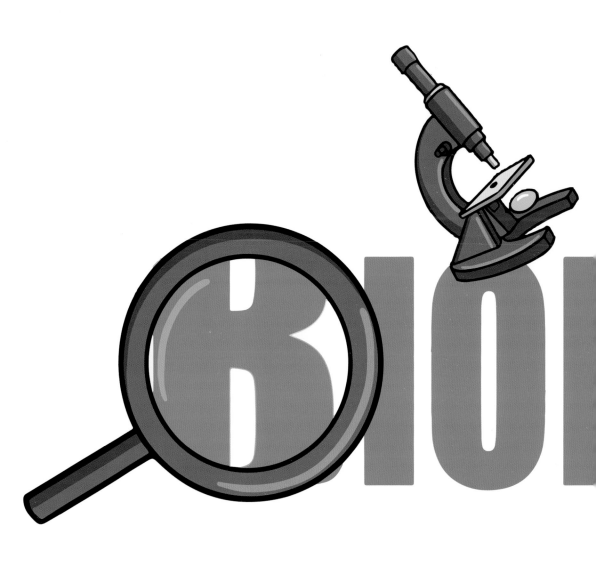

Look at that gut!

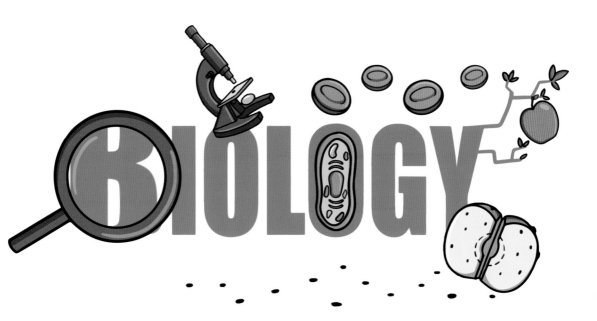

Question: What do you get when you combine fart spray, Bonjela and killer fish? That's right, you get the Biology module at the Ben Phillips School of Pranks! So, listen up, students: if you wanna learn the science of life and the body, and how you can use them to your advantage to prank your mates, you've come to the right place.

When you think about it, the human body is a hotbed of opportunities for pranks, so I thought I'd dedicate a whole chapter of this book to showing you how you can exploit the human body. The lessons in here aren't your usual Biology stuff. For example, there's nothing about the structure of plants. And you won't learn how to make babies – there are already videos on the internet that will show you that. But what you will learn is how to numb your mate's mouth to shut them up, how to give them an unexpected pit wax and then get them spraying fart gas over their armpits. The real stuff... We'll also remember the time I gave Elliot blackfoot and unleashed some hungry fish on his ugly trotters, and then get the lowdown on everyone's favourite pranking old dear – the legendary Nana.

So, put your phone away and pay attention because if I catch you daydreaming or mucking about, I won't think twice about giving you detention!

WAX STRIP SHIRT

You might have noticed that waxing body hair is very popular these days. Some go for the armpits, others for the chest, some even opt for the infamous 'back, sack and crack'. So, in today's class, I'm gonna teach you how to inflict a cheeky pit wax on your bro, whether they want one or not. Think carefully and play this one on someone who deserves it (and who's got enough hair!).

Get it right and you'll absolutely sail through this test, but if you don't take it seriously, you'll fail – and that really will be the pits!

1 Swipe your mate's favourite shirt. You know the one – the one that they love to wear. Every day. EVERY. BLOODY. DAY.

2 Sew wax strips into the underarm areas of the shirt, leaving the wax strips exposed.

3 Casually hang the shirt back up in their wardrobe and wait for them to get ready!

4 When they get home and are about to take their shirt off, sarcastically compliment them on their freshly waxed pits. They'll soon know what you're going on about!

PRANK RATING

Difficulty: 4 out of 5
Hilarity: 4 out of 5
Cost: 1 out of 5
Preparation: 4 out of 5
Danger: 2 out of 5
Mess: 2 out of 5

WAX STRIP SHIRT

ELLIOT'S USED MY RAZOR AGAIN?! GROSS!!

A LITTLE WAXING WILL TEACH HIM NOT TO USE MY RAZOR AGAIN

LAST TIME YOU'LL USE MY STUFF

YAAAAAAAAWWN

AH! OW! AHHHHH!

UGH WHAT?! WHY DOES THIS FEEL SO STICKY?!

AHHHH!!!!

BEEEEEEEEN!!

FART GAS TOWEL

I wanted to come up with a prank any of us can use on that person in our lives who stinks the place out, year in, year out. In my world, that person is someone called Elliot Giles. Believe me, the guy is basically waging a war on my nostrils and it makes me wanna

PUKE! When I played this one on him it came off perfectly.

So, if you're looking for a prank to play on your smelliest mate, this one trumps them all!

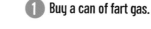 **1** Buy a can of fart gas.

2 Spray it over your victim's bathroom towel.

3 Wait for them to take a shower.

4 When they come out, tell them they smell worse than when they went in!

PRANK RATING

Difficulty: 2 out of 5
Hilarity: 5 out of 5
Cost: 1 out of 5
Preparation: 3 out of 5
Danger: 1 out of 5
Mess: 4 out of 5

TEACHER PROFILE: NANA

Last time she smiled was in 1951

Name: Nana

Position: Head of Biology

Prank experience: Try and find someone more experienced than me – I'll wait!

Teaching style: Step out of line and I'll show you who the boss is!

Number of pranks successfully committed: I lost count at the first million.

Leading victim: By the time you get to my age, everyone ticks you off, and my time is ticking.

Favourite prank tool: I've always said you get a nice kick out of laxatives.

Strictness rating: Hardcore – you're never too old to go over my knee.

Special powers: My hands. If all else fails during a prank, I just give someone a slap.

Funniest thing that happened in class: When we did a dissection class, I gave everyone a dead rat to cut open, but when I got to Elliot, I told him we'd be cutting him open too! The daft bugger believed me and off he ran and hid. We didn't hear from him for weeks – Ben LOVED it!

Top tip: Don't be a snowflake: if you're gonna do a prank, give it some WELLY!

Inspiration: 50 Cent.

Most likely to say: 'Elliot – GET OUT, YOU PERVERT!'

Least likely to say: 'I love you.'

NUMBING TOOTHPASTE

People who won't shut their cakeholes are the worst! So why play just one prank on them when you can play two? In Cooking (page 56), I taught you the Chilli Ice Cream trick for the person in your life who won't shut up, and now we're gonna target them again.

So, if your first strike didn't do the business, here's another chance to get your own back on that blabbermouth. And believe me, if this one doesn't shut them up, nothing will. We're gonna take them down!

Originally, I wanted to play this one on Elliot, but there was one problem — I had to wait for him to brush his teeth, which is something he only does every few months. GROSS! So, for me the gap between steps three and four was long — even longer than one of his boring stories — but it was worth waiting for. I numbed that guy's mouth so well, he didn't speak for days. I could almost hear myself think — it was AWESOME!

But before you rush into the toothpaste prank, first brush up on how it works...

1. Get a tube of Bonjela and find your mate's tube of toothpaste. (If your friend's anything like Elliot, this could be quite a hunt! You'll probably find it on the floor, covered in dust and cobwebs.)

2. Remove the lid from the toothpaste and squeeze a generous amount of Bonjela into the tube.

3. Put the toothpaste back in the correct place, hide the Bonjela and wait!

4. For extra marks, film your bro as they dribble uncontrollably after brushing their teeth!

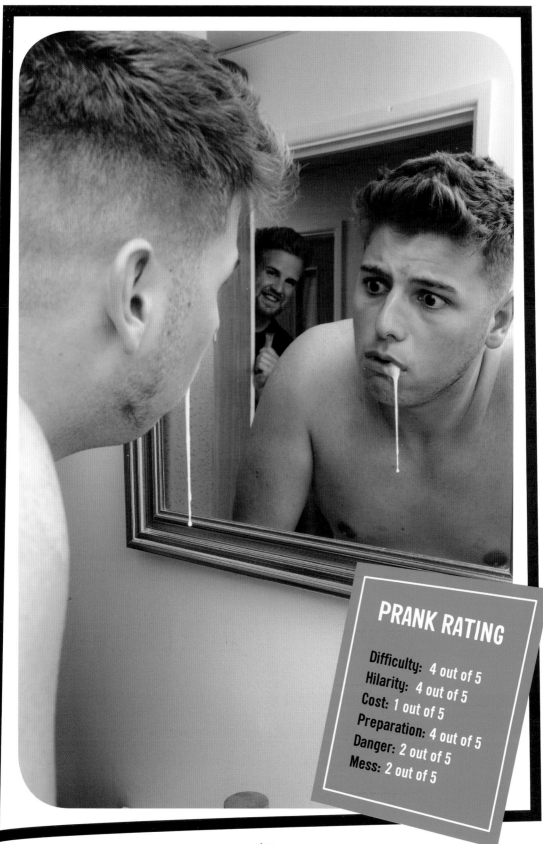

PRANK RATING

Difficulty: 4 out of 5
Hilarity: 4 out of 5
Cost: 1 out of 5
Preparation: 4 out of 5
Danger: 2 out of 5
Mess: 2 out of 5

HISTORY LESSONS WITH GRANDAD

WALL OF FAME:
THE BLACKFOOT PRANK

Here's a bit of classic Biology for you – the time we turned Elliot's foot black and then unleashed some killer fish on him! Mastering this double whammy teaches you important skills: the art of luring a victim into a trap as well as keeping your hands and nerves steady as they sleep.

This is one of my all-time favourites. To pull it off was quite a 'FEET' but Ben 'TOE-tally nailed' it – I was so proud of him!

While Elliot was asleep, Ben sprayed his foot black.

Elliot woke up and thought he'd got actual blackfoot!

I told him a simple fish pedicure would see it gone in seconds. He took the bait – literally!

So, we took him along to a Turkish barber for a fish pedicure. He wasn't sure at first, but once he knew there was a cup of tea on the way, he plunged in!

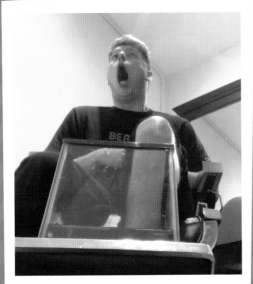

Within seconds he wished he hadn't because the fish bit properly into his feet.

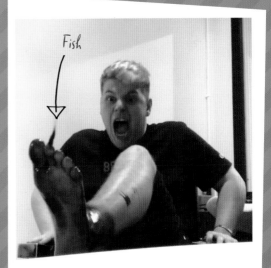

Fish

It's safe to say that he didn't enjoy having fish on his feet!

Headmaster Ben
Hero.

Manager Adam
Length: Two weeks' detention.
Reason: For coming to school
with tattoos, an attitude and
THAT haircut!

PE is one part of school you never forget: the smelly kit, the knackering runs through the woods, the angry teacher shouting his head off at you, and then ... the SHOWERS! These horrors stay with you forever – it's like they're burned into your brain. Well, the PE classes at the School of Pranks are gonna be just as challenging and memorable but trust me, they'll be way more fun, too.

I've got three awesome pranks for you to learn. With the Nerf Gun Superglue prank you'll be able to cover your friend in sticky bullets, the Ink Whistle trick lets you make your PE teacher look the tool they are, and, just when you thought it was safe to go back in the water, along comes my Poo Pool game!

The fitter your body, the fitter your mind will be – and a sharp mind is essential for any prankster. You need to stay one step ahead of the people you are targeting, after all. So, make sure you take this chapter seriously. The more you put in, the more you'll take out – so get ready to work up a sweat!

NERF GUN SUPERGLUE

Do you wanna be a good prankster ... or do you wanna be a GREAT prankster? If you wanna be up there among the greats, you have to learn to take your jokes one step further.

Take the Nerf Gun ... anyone can sneak up on their friends and pummel them with Nerf bullets. It's a decent prank: there's the element of surprise, the moment of shock for the target and it's just a mega laugh. But what if you took it to another level? That's exactly what you can do here. By bringing superglue into the mix, you can turn a good prank into a great one. So, here's where we'll sort the quality from the rest: if you smash it, I'll know you're serious.

1. Buy a Nerf Gun, extra bullets and superglue. Yes, it's an investment but trust me, you'll get your return in LOLZ!

2. Apply superglue to the tip of the Nerf bullets and load up the gun.

3. Ambush your mate with the Nerf Gun and watch the bullets stick!

4. To top it all off, snap a cheeky picture of them and post it on your Instagram. As headmaster, I'll be paying close attention to your account to see how you fare.

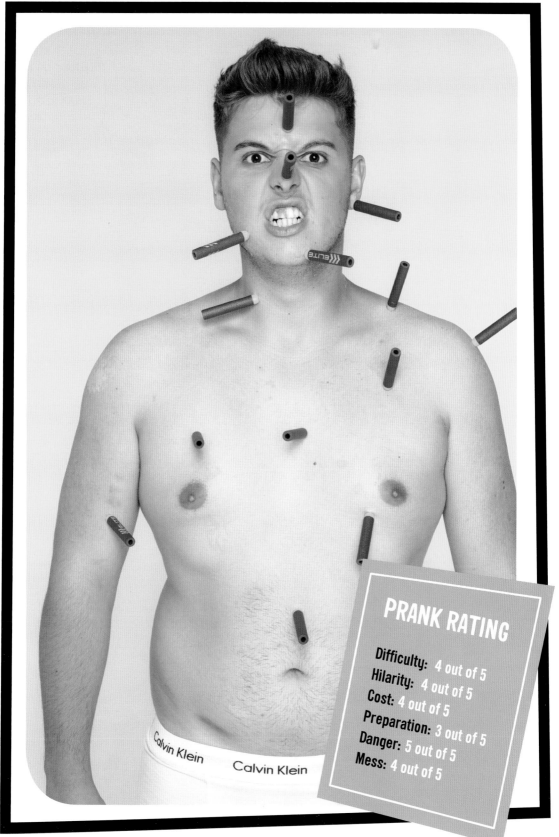

PRANK RATING

Difficulty: 4 out of 5
Hilarity: 4 out of 5
Cost: 4 out of 5
Preparation: 3 out of 5
Danger: 5 out of 5
Mess: 4 out of 5

POO POOL

Have you seen those videos on YouTube where someone accidentally does a poo in a swimming pool or Jacuzzi? The water suddenly turns brown around the culprit and everyone else sprints out of the tub like, like someone's pooed in the pool — what could be worse than that?

Imagine how you'd feel if you were that person. You'd want to literally die of embarrassment, right? So, I thought I'd come up with a way for you to put your friend in exactly that position minus the real poo, cos.

that's just GROSS! The best part of this prank is that no one will believe your bro when they say they haven't done a poo. Because that's exactly what they would say, right?

This is one of the funniest pranks you can pull on anyone. Trust me, it's INCREDIBLE. When I played it on Elliot (photos here) it took him months to live it down, so make sure you keep it for someone really special.

Okay, guys, it's time to make a splash. A massive BROWN SPLASH (this I like)!

1 Steal your friend's swimming shorts.

2 Get some Oxo or gravy browning cubes and place a couple in the pockets.

3 Put the shorts back and wait for your mate to go swimming.

4 Watch the horror on their fellow swimmers' faces as everyone thinks they've pooed in the pool! Don't forget to get pics for the thumbnail, if you're uploading.

PRANK RATING

Difficulty: 1 out of 5
Hilarity: 5 out of 5
Cost: 1 out of 5
Preparation: 2 out of 5
Danger: 1 out of 5
Mess: Infinity out of 5

TEACHER PROFILE:
TRISTAN

Have you checked out my Instagram?

Name: Tristan	**Strictness rating:** Are you joking? With a face like this you don't need the heavy stuff! * Winks *
Position: Head of PE	
Prank experience: I may not be able to keep up with Ben and Grandad, but at least I've got a six-pack, not a fat pack.	**Special powers:** Erm? Hello?!
Teaching style: Step out of line and I'll show you who the boss is!	**Funniest thing that happened in class:** Before a swimming lesson, Elliot asked me if it was true that the pool turned green around you if you took a wee in there. I told him this was a myth and the rest is history.
Number of pranks successfully committed: Ask anyone in South Africa, I've racked up some numbers.	**Top tip:** When in doubt, work out!
Leading victim: Cameraman Carl.	**Inspiration:** Ben. OBVIOUSLY. One day, I'll rule this school.
Favourite prank tool: Water — you can surf on it, but you can also throw it over someone (Elliot) while they're sleeping.	**Most likely to say:** 'Have you checked out my Instagram?'
	Least likely to say: 'No time for a shower, Elliot.'

INK WHISTLE

What is it about PE teachers? They're the noisiest people on the entire planet. Every lesson, they shout their heads off, clap their hands, and they keep blowing that stupid whistle. All it does is echo off the walls of the hall, giving everyone a blinding headache. And why are they so angry? Bet Elliot would make a great PE teacher!

It's time to turn the tables and teach them a lesson they'll NEVER forget.

This is the perfect school prank because you can find the equipment you need for it inside any school building. You'll also need steady hands and plenty of nerve, but if you get this one right, you'll have everyone in stitches. Well, everyone apart from the PE teacher, obvs. They'll be absolutely livid and will probably turn the air blue in more ways than one. So, don't expect to get away lightly. Remember: if you play a prank, you have to accept payback.

1 Get hold of your PE teacher's whistle.

2 Crack open an ink cartridge and pour the ink inside the whistle.

3 Put the whistle back where they left it and wait for it to blow up in their face!

4 Expect to receive detention. AT LEAST! And the adulation of your bros.

#144

PRANK RATING

Difficulty: 3 out of 5
Hilarity: 4 out of 5
Cost: 1 out of 5
Preparation: 4 out of 5
Danger: 5 out of 5
Mess: 5 out of 5

INK WHISTLE

HISTORY LESSONS WITH GRANDAD

WALL OF FAME:
AB BELT WORKOUT

Some people who don't like exercise try and take a shortcut to getting beach body ready. When Elliot attempted this, Ben stitched him up like a kipper. As soon as he heard that Elliot was buying an ab belt, he swiped it, interfered with it, and gave that guy a workout he'll NEVER forget!

We took a trip to the shops to buy a solder iron.

Ben took the belt's control panel off and carefully located the correct capacitor.

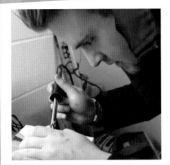

And then he burned it off, so the belt's limit shot from a safe 12 volts to 100 or more. In short, when Elliot put it on, it was gonna go OFF THE SCALE!

That's exactly how it played out – Elliot said his abs were 'on fire'!

In no time at all, it was all getting a bit much for him …

… but that boy was determined to get his six-pack.

'This thing is giving me grief!!!'

Then he wore it to the shops – which didn't go as well as he had hoped!

His agony continued into the evening.

Eventually, Ben found him hiding down an alley. 'Just get out – I'm having a poo!' Elliot cried.

ELLIOT'S DIARY: SPORTS DAY

Since the day I joined the School of Pranks I've been teased non-stop. Thanks to Ben, I've spent most of the time being pointed at and laughed at. Got no friends. Got no girlfriend. So, I was determined to do well at Sports Day. Here was my chance to impress everyone, or at least take the heat off me for a day. I'd show Ben he'd messed with the wrong guy!

I've got a tubby build, so I really fancied my chances at the tug of war. When I was lining up for it, Ben came over and told me he thought I'd be a 'natural' – 'After all, you like a good tug, don't you?' We'll see who has the last laugh, Ben!

He put me at the end of the rope, I gripped hard and prepared to pull. But I immediately slithered off the end of the rope. Ben stood there laughing, shouting: 'Butterfingers!' GAAAAH!

Next, the egg and spoon race. As we were lining up, Ben came over and switched my egg for a new one. I didn't have time to ask him why because the race started. Halfway through, I felt a foot trip me up and I crashed to the ground, breaking my egg. And that's when the smell started. It was SO rank! It smelt like something had died. No, it smelt like EVERYTHING ON THE PLANET had died. Everyone ran off in different directions, people's eyes and noses were streaming, even birds were flying away in a panic.

After the smell passed, there was time for just one more event – the boot-throwing contest. My chance to make everything good! Again, Ben was there to hand me my equipment. He passed me a boot and I prepared to hurl it as far as I could.

The boot felt weirdly heavy but I was so angry by this point that I flung it as far as I could. It flew into the watching crowd and showered them with liquid. As they were drying themselves off, they started sniffing and they suddenly got really angry.

Before I knew it, I had a wee-covered mob charging at me. I ran away so fast I could have beaten Usain Bolt!

I HATE sports!

I HATE sports!

I HATE sports!

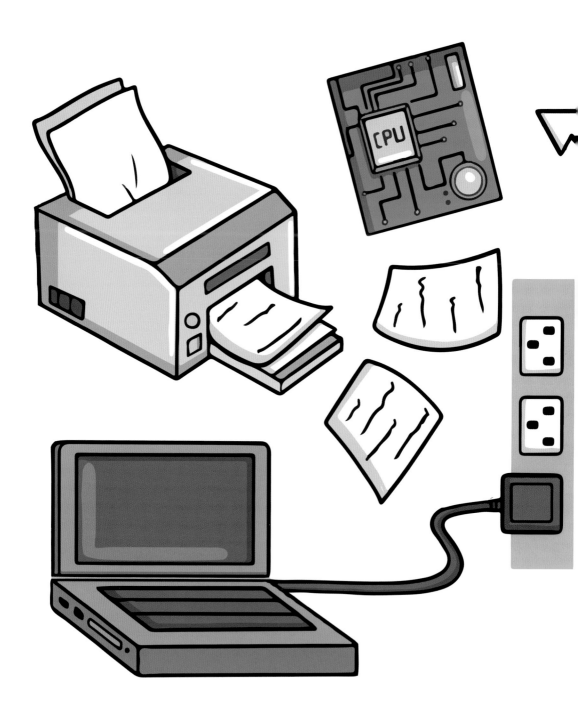

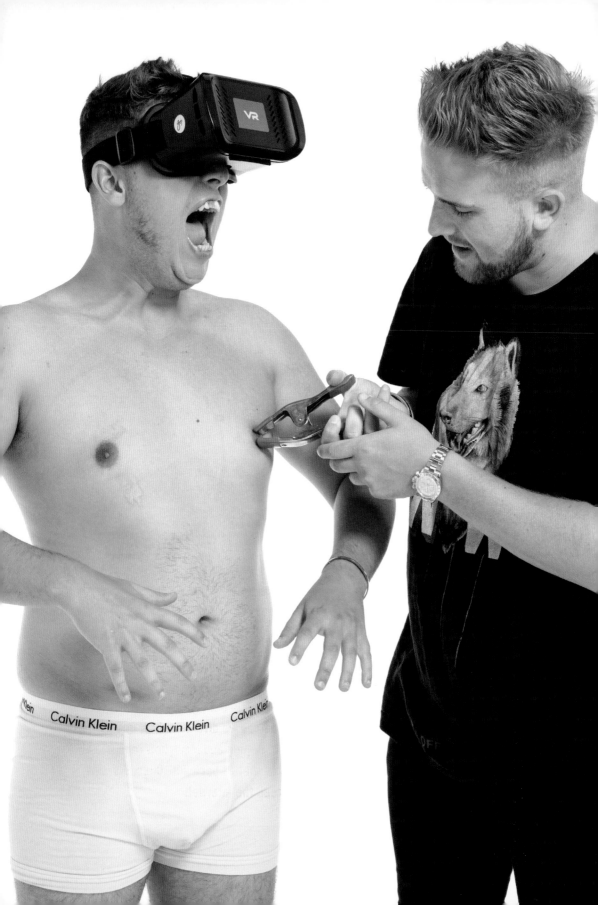

In case you were thinking IT's all about fixing laptops and wearing nerdy T-shirts ... you're so wrong, bro! The internet is AMAZING – it brought us our fans and can be your chance to go viral. The possibilities are endless.

Here, at the School of Pranks, I want to help you create videos that'll have you laughing for days and get the world laughing with you. Take the Bluetooth Headphone Trap prank... In the days before Bluetooth, if you were bored on a flight, you'd have to put chilli sauce in your mate's snoring mouth! PlayStations and VR headsets didn't exist when Nana was first knocking around but now we're free to use both these gadgets for some serious madness.

As well as teaching you three tricks, I'll also give you a bit more on my useless bro, Elliot, including what happened at Parents' Evening and everything you want to know (and some things you DON'T!) about him. Then Grandad will be back to reminisce about another prank from the vaults – this time the Flipper Feet. So, get ready as we dive head first into modern technology and learn how to go digital on your mate's backside. Guys, it's time to break the internet!

VIRTUAL REALITY

Look at a senior prankster like Grandad and imagine the changes he's seen during his lifetime. When he was born, there was no such thing as a mobile phone, things like virtual reality were unheard of and the most advanced technology they had was a black and white TV with only one channel. ONE CHANNEL! Can you believe that? But a good prankster like him doesn't just adapt to every new thing that comes along, they actively work out how to use every modern invention for new ways to cause mischief.

That's where this prank comes in. The virtual reality headset is the perfect tool for you to use on your mate when you want a laugh. I used this one on Elliot and he freaked out so much, he nearly wet himself. And when I say 'nearly', I mean 'actually did'!

This one takes a bit of upfront investment but you can always see if someone you know can lend you some of the equipment. To return the favour, you could even invite them to come along and watch it unfold!

1 First, you need to line up the equipment so get a virtual reality headset, a litter picker or washing line pegs and a leaf blower or a hairdryer.

2 Convince your friend to try out your new, awesome virtual reality headset. Really lay it on and tell them they won't believe how realistic it is!

3 While your mate is in the middle of the virtual reality experience – maybe they're about to enter a room where a zombie could be or have just crept into a dragon's lair in *Skyrim* – use the litter picker to pinch parts of their body and turn on the hairdryer suddenly to scare the crap out of them! (Make sure you time it right with the video, or better still, a Facebook live!)

4 Expect to receive detention. AT LEAST! And the adulation of your bros.

PRANK RATING

Difficulty: 4 out of 5
Hilarity: 4 out of 5
Cost: 5 out of 5
Preparation: 2 out of 5
Danger: 2 out of 5
Mess: 2 out of 5

PLAYSTATION TIMER

We all love sitting down on the PlayStation. You can tear it up on *Grand Theft Auto*, freak out on *The Last of Us* or own it on *Fortnite Battle Royale* … it's a sick way to kill a bit of time.

Notice I said a *bit* of time, not *all* your time. You don't wanna become a PlayStation junkie like Elliot. The guy spends every waking minute of his day and night glued to the screen and will bore the arse off everyone about levels, rewards and points.

If you've got a mate like this, and are willing to put in a small investment, you can teach them a lesson they won't forget in a hurry. They'll tell you there's nothing more annoying than when you lose a game just as you were about to win. So, here's what you need to do…

1 Get down to your local electronics store and buy a timer plug.

2 Set a time for it to turn off during the peak times your friend is usually smashing it on their games console.

3 Connect it all together and wait for them to sit down and play.

4 Watch them rage as their console unexpectedly turns off mid-game!

Ha ha! Game Over!

PRANK RATING

Difficulty: 1 out of 5
Hilarity: 4 out of 5
Cost: 4 out of 5
Preparation: 2 out of 5
Danger: 1 out of 5
Mess: Zero out of 5

PUPIL
PROFILE:
ELLIOT

Name: Elliot Giles

Prank experience: Name a prank and I've had it played on me, like 300 times. It's getting ridiculous now!

Favourite place at school: None of it, I hate the place!

Number of pranks I've had played on me: TOO MANY!

Leading tormentor: BEN, of course! What are you, an idiot?

Favourite lesson: I like PE, don't have to spell or write.

Intellectual rating: I'm much cleverer than Ben.

Special powers: I seem to be able to survive anything. Which is good, given what Ben puts me through!

Funniest thing that happened in class: Nothing funny EVER happens in any class. It's NEVER funny when the joke is on you and the joke is on me EVERY BLOODY TIME!

Top tip: Don't bother trying to escape from Ben. I got so sick of him, I once tried to move to the moon, but NASA said they wouldn't take me. Screw them, I'll build my own rocket again!

Inspiration: Thanos — he can kill anyone he likes.

Least likely to say: 'I like school.'

Most likely to say: 'BENNNNNNNN!'

BLUETOOTH HEADPHONE TRAP

Catching a flight to another country is one of my favourite things to do. The excitement of visiting new places, meeting new people and learning about pranking around the world is AMAZING, but the flight itself is one of the MOST BORING. For hours on end you're stuck in your seat, the food tastes like CRAP and you've already watched all the films (and if you're really unlucky, you're sitting next to Elliot!). Then, when you turn to talk to your friend because you need a distraction, they've fallen asleep. Well, here's your chance to give them the biggest shock of their life. As you'll see, the first part of this prank is downloading scary noises. Think which noise will most unsettle your friend. If they've watched lots of scary films, a ghost noise will do the trick. If they're scared of flying, find one that sounds like a plane crashing. You'll have them running down the aisle...

Get inside their head and make this one go with a BANG!

1. Before your flight, download some scary loud sounds that are available to play while on airplane mode.

2. Wait for your friend to fall asleep on the flight.

3. Connect to their Bluetooth headphones.

4. Play the scary loud noises through their headphones and wait for them to wake up and freak out! It's BRILLIANT!

PRANK RATING

Difficulty: 1 out of 5
Hilarity: 4 out of 5
Cost: 2 out of 5
Preparation: 2 out of 5
Danger: 1 out of 5
Mess: Zero out of 5

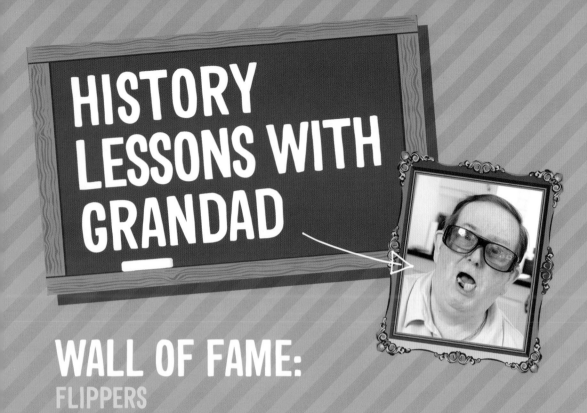

HISTORY LESSONS WITH GRANDAD

WALL OF FAME:
FLIPPERS

This was a cracker. Ben decided to superglue a pair of diving flippers to Elliot's feet. At least it contained his awful-smelling feet for a while.

It's a good prank to revisit because as well as being pant-wettingly funny, it shows how you can take a throwaway remark someone has made and turn it against them as a classic prank.

Here's what went down...

Me and Carl went out and bought a pair of flippers and a snorkel

We waited until Elliot was asleep...

...and poured superglue into the flippers

We then pushed the flippers onto his feet so they stuck.

We'd also superglued the snorkel and put that on him too.

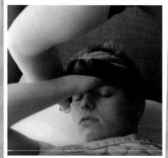

Then using strong tape we stuck his hand to his head.

He was not happy when he woke up!

Not happy at all!

He couldn't get dressed so we dressed him

We took him for a drive

And clothes shopping.

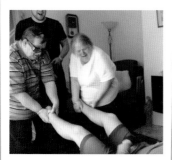

Me and Nana had no sympathy – we pulled him off the sofa

But Nana did feed him some beans, with the old 'choo choo train' method

The police even turned up – classic prank.

PARENTS' EVENING

Parents' Evening — every kid's worst nightmare. Especially Elliot's. Well, if you sit there all year, picking your nose, it's not gonna be much fun, is it?

When Mum and Dad sat down, I told them that Elliot was a complete donk, who can't even understand the basics. They believed me, but I tested him anyway: 'Elliot, what's two plus two?'

He couldn't answer.

So, then I asked: 'Elliot, can you spell "dog"?'

Again, he had no answer. What an IDIOT!

Then I told them: 'Unfortunately, I also have to tell you that there have been a lot of complaints made about Elliot's personal hygiene.' At this stage, Nana wandered past and casually rolled a stink bomb underneath Elliot's chair — ha-ha, she's a legend! As the stench filled the air, everyone got up to leave — except Elliot, who was superglued to his chair. Nice one, Tristan!

Sorry, bro!

SCHOOL TRIP

Is your packed lunch ready? Got an anorak in case it rains? Are you ready to walk in twos? Good, it's time for the school trip! You're nearing the end of your year at the School of Pranks, so as a treat, I'm taking us all out and about.

Most teachers are a bit nervous on school trips because they're terrified they'll accidentally lose one of the kids. But on our school trip, it's the PUPILS who are scared. Even when we're not at school, the teachers are still schooling the students in the art of pranking.

So, here's three more pranks for you to learn and put into practice out in the field. Poo Plane will have your travelling mate sprinting to the toilets, while Superglue Luggage has your smug holidaymaker well and truly stuck. Then finally, Farty Flight guarantees the loudest flight you've ever had!

We'll also take a peek at Elliot's report card. It's fair to say I don't think he'll take many happy memories from his year at the school! At least he can have a bit of fun on the school trip – or we can have a bit of fun with him...

POO PLANE

Ever gone on a long journey with Elliot? I've been on several and I can tell you this for nothing: that guy's up and down like a yo-yo! Whether he's on a train, plane or in a car, he wants to get up and stretch his legs every five minutes.

It's made me so angry over the years that I created a prank to show him what it's like when you're just relaxing on a flight and

someone – or in this case, something – drives you round the bend. So, make sure you play this one on the annoying travel companion in your world!

Anyone who's travelled a bit knows there are good flights and bad flights in life. Well, get this prank right and your mate's about to have the crappiest flight of their life!

1. Buy a bag of boiled sweets and some laxatives the same colour as the sweets.

2. Remove some of the sweets from their wrappers and replace them with laxatives.

3. Place them back in the bag and on the flight, offer them to your friend to help with take-off.

4. Yep, you've guessed it: this one's gonna be EXPLOSIVE!

PRANK RATING

Difficulty: 2 out of 5
Hilarity: 4 out of 5
Cost: 2 out of 5
Preparation: 3 out of 5
Danger: 2 out of 5
Mess: 5 out of 5

SUPERGLUE LUGGAGE

Apply superglue all over the handles

This one really needs no introduction: it's simple, it's brilliant ... and it makes Elliot so MAD!

1. Wait for your mate to pack his or her suitcase.

2. Get hold of some superglue and apply it all over the handles.

3. Wait for your friend to grab their suitcase and head out of the door on the way to a nice, relaxing beach.

4. Watch the horror on their face as they realise they can't let go.

5. Tell them to be more careful in future and walk away, laughing!

PRANK RATING

Difficulty: 2 out of 5
Hilarity: 4 out of 5
Cost: 1 out of 5
Preparation: 3 out of 5
Danger: 3 out of 5
Mess: 3 out of 5

BEN AND ELLIOT AT SCHOOL!

#179

FARTY FLIGHT

We've all got that one mate with the most annoying wind issue of all. Yes, I'm talking about the SNEAKY FARTER, the SLY TRUMPER, the SILENT VIOLENT ... I know who mine is. His stomach pumps out gas night and day, without making any noise. Then he sits there with an innocent expression on his face as if the nasty stench has nothing to do with him!

People like Elliot make me sick, so I came up with this prank to help you get them back...

1. Get a small Bluetooth speaker and sneakily pack it in your mate's hand luggage, making sure your phone is connected.

2. Download some fart noises onto your phone. I recommend a proper spread – some high-pitched wails, a few standard trumps and perhaps a couple of wet ones.

3. After take-off, crank up the volume to full and blast those farts so everyone in the cabin can hear.

4. Turn around and stare at your mate in disgust. Say out loud: 'Look, I know you're a nervous flier, but you're bang out of order. If you can't control yourself, go to the toilet!'

5. For added humiliation, call over a flight attendant and tell them your friend seems to have had a little accident. Ask loudly if they have any wet wipes.

PRANK RATING

Difficulty: 2 out of 5
Hilarity: 5 out of 5
Cost: 1 out of 5
Preparation: 4 out of 5
Danger: 2 out of 5
Mess: 1 out of 5

HISTORY LESSONS WITH GRANDAD

WALL OF FAME:
PLUNGER

Have you ever seen someone doing the Walk of Shame, Stride of Pride (or whatever you youngsters call it) when they've stayed out all night? You see them staggering home at six in the morning, still dolled up in their party gear. In the latest instalment of our classic pranks, we remember when Ben gave Elliot his very own Walk of Shame.

It's safe to say that when the general public saw Elliot this way, their opinion of him took a plunge – if that's at all possible!

Ben grabbed a load of plungers from his local hardware store.

He went round to Marge's, where Elliot was having a kip, and started applying superglue to the plungers.

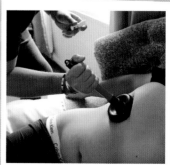

Then he started sticking the plungers to Elliot's body.

We wanted one stuck to his knob, so we let Marge do that one.

Elliot woke up and got a right shock!

Marge called Elliot a 'pervert' again and yanked off one of the plungers. That's gotta hurt!

Time for the 'plunged pervert' to face the outside world!

Elliot demanded to go to Tesco to look for a hacksaw, but all he got was weird looks!

He went to work at the bingo and got the sack! Apparently, turning up to your job with a plunger stuck to your head is against the rules. Who knew?

He even went to church – often a sign of a man in crisis!

This looks bad. I was trying to pull the plunger off, NOT trying to pull Elliot off – honest!

Ben tried to knock off the plunger using my walking stick and then he removed the rest by hand.

But it backfired!

ELLIOT'S

REPORT CARD

It has been quite an experience getting to know your son this year.

We very much hoped that the angry, confused young man who arrived on day one would blossom into a calmer character and a grade-A student. Who am I trying to kid? We knew that wasn't going to happen! Unfortunately, Elliot's obsession with me held back his progress throughout the year. Any misfortune that happened in his life he blamed on me, but we never found any evidence to support his wild accusations.

Are we honestly expected to believe that our most respected member of staff poured a bucket of pig poo over Elliot? And would a busy teacher even have the time to hide laxatives in Elliot's lunch on a daily basis? We all know it's just him trying to get attention.

Putting aside these crazy conspiracy theories, we were also disappointed to note how much time Elliot spent hiding in the toilets rather than in the classroom. Well, at least that made a change from the hours spent stomping the playing fields in his pants, ranting angrily about me stealing his clothes. He found making friends almost as challenging as learning.

Given that he was too nervous to pay attention in class and therefore failed every exam he sat, we have to say the prospects for Elliot seem bleak. The best he can hope for is 45 years as a dog walker and professional poo collector, provided he can overcome his notorious hygiene issues. Even the dogs have standards!

I would keep Elliot back, but I just don't want him here any more.

Sincerely,
Ben
Headmaster, School of Pranks

p.s. Sorry Bro!

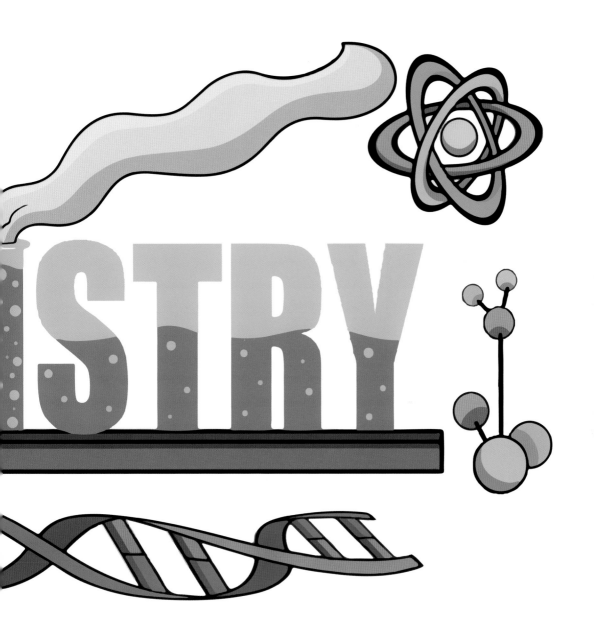

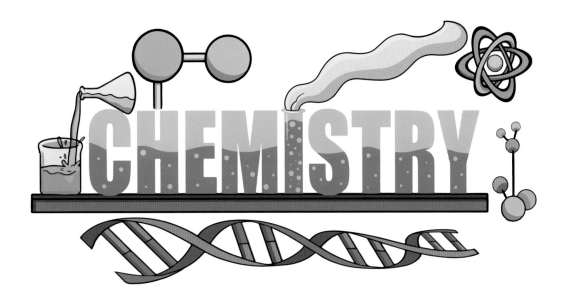

CHEMISTRY

Ah, chemistry – if you like pranks, this is the lesson that has you properly buzzing. Let's face it – anything you need safety goggles for is great for some serious mischief.

Whether it's the Bunsen burners, test tubes, lethal chemicals or the gas pipes – there's potential for chaos everywhere you look. Does any other subject offer more opportunities to mess things up?

It's really, really fun. You're not sweating your way through confusing sums or yawning at boring poems. You're literally talking bangs, flames and fizzes. Science is awesome and that's why it's super-exciting to step out of the classroom and into the lab.

In this section, I'll take you through some of the best chemistry-related pranks. With the Mentos and Coke trick you'll learn how to make a bottle blow up in your victim's face. In the Stink Bomb Brakes you can get your own back on any driver and leave them puking their guts out.

Finally, with Colouring Comforter you can redesign someone's entire clothing collection in just one wash. That's proper chemical warfare right there.

I hope you're pumped because it's time to take your learning to a new level. So if you're serious about smashing it, put on your lab coat, get your safety goggles on and prepare to blow things up.

COLOURING COMFORTER

You know what? I think Elliot must have missed out on a lot of life's lessons. Take his clothes … I swear that guy hardly manages to wash or feed himself some days. Also, he doesn't seem to realise you're supposed to mix up what you wear. I don't think he's ever updated his look, it's just the same combo every day – baggy T-shirt and jeans. One outfit for life … he's like the Simon Cowell of Wales!

I got so bored of seeing him in the same clobber every day, I decided that if he wouldn't update his image, I'd have to do it for him. And that, my pranking pupils, is how I came up with this, a proper messy trick to play – I absolutely love it!

1. Buy some food colouring (make sure it's the same colour as your clothes-wash comforter).

2. Wait until your mate is out, then carefully add the food colouring to the comforter. Give it a good shake and put the bottle back in the cupboard.

3. Wait for your mate to put a clothes wash on. (If you get bored waiting, each time they come into the room, drop hints about something smelling bad!)

4. When the wash cycle is finished, watch their face as they remove their clothes from the machine and realise they've got an unexpected fresh new wardrobe!

%#!$&

PRANK RATING

Difficulty: 1 out of 5
Hilarity: 4 out of 5
Cost: 1 out of 5
Preparation: 1 out of 5
Danger: 2 out of 5
Mess: 5 out of 5

STINK BOMB BRAKES

Normally, the best part of a prank is watching it all kick off. It's unreal when all that planning comes off. But this is a prank you probably won't wanna be around for – if you haven't guessed from the title, you'll see why in a minute.

Stink bombs have been around for a long, long time. Grandad was using them way back in the day, and because they're so powerful, we're still using them in the 21st century. So, I thought I'd find a way that you can use them on someone without having to put up with that horrible smell yourself. This is what I came up with. Now it's your chance to use Chemistry's greatest invention to transform your mate's car into the smelliest place on the planet.

1. Get hold of some stink bombs and some tape or glue.

2. Gain access to your mate's car. You might need to swipe their keys when they're not looking, or tell them you left something in there.

3. Superglue or tape a stink bomb or two to their brake pedal (that way, they get a little bit down the road before they realise).

4. Lock the car and act like nothing has happened – like butter wouldn't melt in your mouth.

5. Keep your phone switched on and wait for the angry call.

PRANK RATING

Difficulty: 3 out of 5
Hilarity: 4 out of 5
Cost: 1 out of 5
Preparation: 2 out of 5
Danger: 5 out of 5
Mess: 5 out of 5

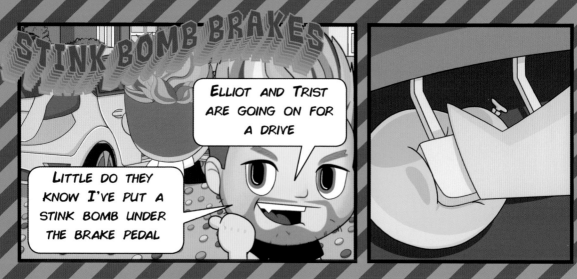

TEACHER PROFILE: GEORGIA

Don't let that smile fool you for a moment

Name: Georgia	**Funniest thing that happened in class:** When Elliot farted just as the Bunsen burners were lit. The whole lab was set on fire and the entire class ran screaming into the playground in flames. It was like something from a war zone.
Position: Head of Chemistry	
Prank experience: 23 years	
Teaching style: Deceptively strict – don't let that smile fool you for a moment.	**Top tip:** Don't be scared to mix random chemicals together – what's the worst that could happen? ... Elliot.
Number of pranks successfully committed: None of your business.	
Leading victim: Ben – treat them mean keep them keen.	**Inspiration:** Kim K, Kourtney Kardashian, Khloe Kardashian, Kylie Jenner, Kendall Jenner, Kris Jenner... did I mention Kim K?
Favourite prank tool: Dazzling smile.	**Most likely to say:** 'Do you like my new hair?'
Strictness rating: 10 out of 10	**Least likely to say:** 'I'm having a no make-up day.'
Special powers: The ability to make every experiment literally blow up in your face.	

MENTOS AND COKE PRANK

We all know that one person who's addicted to fizzy drinks. Morning, noon and night they're either swigging on a bottle of Coke, burping like a frog, peeing like a horse or wondering how the hell their belly got so massive.

In my world, that person is Elliot. He got so fat and belchy I couldn't take it any more. I'm sure you know someone the same. Here's how to get your own back...

1. Buy some Mentos and a big bottle of Coke. And I mean big – the bigger the bottle the funnier the prank will be.

2. Pop a handful of Mentos out of the packet and hide them in your hand.

3. Take the Coke bottle over to your victim and present it to them. If they're a proper fizz-junkie then they won't suspect a thing; they'll be too busy drooling like a dog at the bubbles to come.

4. Face it, it's not going to take them long to open the bottle, and once they do, it's time to move fast. Distract them and put as many Mentos as possible into the top. You may only get time for three or four but ram in as many of those babies as you can.

5. Right... now it's time to move even faster. Run to a safe distance and watch as the bottle explodes in their face. Or just sit, watch and laugh.

Put as many Mentos as possible into the top

The bigger the bottle the funnier the prank will be

PRANK RATING

Difficulty: 2 out of 5
Hilarity: 4 out of 5
Cost: 2 out of 5
Preparation: 1 out of 5
Danger: 3 out of 5
Mess: 4 out of 5

Mentos and Coke

TAKE SOME MENTOS AND COLA

FIZZ FIZZ

POP IN SOME MENTOS TO FIZZ UP THE COLA

CLOSE THE BOTTLE QUICK!

NOW YOU'VE GOT A PRANK READY FOR SOME VICTIMS

?

AH!

HEY ELLIOT! I WANT SOME!

HUH?

OH NO TRIST! THIS IS MINE!

HISTORY LESSONS WITH GRANDAD

WALL OF FAME:
ULTIMATE FIDGET SPINNER'S PRANK

Ah, I remember this one well! Pay attention because this golden oldie teaches you some major pranking skills. It shows how important it is to have steady hands and to be as quiet as a mouse when pranking someone in their sleep. Plus, it will improve your glue game.

It's also worth learning because it will make you more creative — so follow Ben's example and arrange the fidget spinners in a pretty pattern. (If they look anything like Elliot, you'll be doing them a favour by tarting them up.)

So, stop 'fidgeting' at the back and pay attention to this blast from the past. Here's how it panned out...

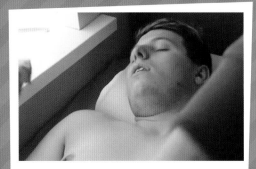

We waited until Elliot was kipping like a baby, getting some of that beauty sleep he so badly needs.

We then put plenty of glue on the back of the fidget spinners and started to stick them to him.

Once we got the first one stuck to Elliot without waking him, we knew we were on to a winner.

So, we went for it big time — we covered that scamp in fidget spinners: his face, his arms, his massive belly — the whole lot!

ELLIOTGILESUK

Then it was time to retreat and wait for him to wake up.

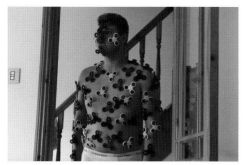

When he got up, the guy was proper angry — we couldn't stop laughing!

And he was none too pleased when he pulled the fidget spinners off him!

As you can see, his mood didn't improve when we took him to Tesco.

Then he got thrown out of the store and banned — again! Honest, we thought our sides were gonna split.

The highlight came when he went out for a selfie with some kid outside and ended up getting attacked. 'They were like piranhas!' he shouted.

#205

GRADUATION CERTIFICATE

The School of Pranks presents this certificate to

_____

For absolutely smashing it in your studies.

You helped me wind up Elliot and you proved that you know your stink bomb from your water bomb.

Congratulations! Now go and unleash some chaos on the world (and particularly your own bro).

Signed _Headmaster Ben_